October Sky

by
Homer H. Hickam, Jr.

Teacher Guide

Written by
Pat Watson

Edited by
Heather M. Johnson

Note

The Dell paperback edition of the book, ©1998 by Homer H. Hickam, Jr., was used to prepare this guide. The page references may differ in other editions.

Please note: This novel deals with sensitive, mature issues. Parts may contain profanity, sexual references, and/or descriptions of violence. Please assess the appropriateness of this book for the age level and maturity of your students prior to reading and discussing it with them.

ISBN 1-58130-816-7

Copyright infringement is a violation of Federal Law.

© 2003, 2004 by Novel Units, Inc., Bulverde, Texas. All rights reserved. No part of this publication may be reproduced, translated, stored in a retrieval system, or transmitted in any way or by any means (electronic, mechanical, photocopying, recording, or otherwise) without prior written permission from Novel Units, Inc.

Photocopying of student worksheets by a classroom teacher at a non-profit school who has purchased this publication for his/her own class is permissible. Reproduction of any part of this publication for an entire school or for a school system, by for-profit institutions and tutoring centers, or for commercial sale is strictly prohibited.

Novel Units is a registered trademark of Novel Units, Inc.

Printed in the United States of America.

To order, contact your local school supply store, or—

Novel Units, Inc.
P.O. Box 97
Bulverde, TX 78163-0097

Web site: www.educyberstor.com

Table of Contents

Summary 3

Background Information 4

About the Author 5

Initiating Activities 6

Thirteen Sections 13
    Each section contains: Summary, Vocabulary,
    Discussion Questions, and Supplementary Activities

Post-reading Discussion Questions 34

Post-reading Extension Activities 36

Assessment 37

Glossary 38

Skills and Strategies

Comprehension
    Cause/effect, evaluation, compare/contrast

Literary Elements
    Characterization, metaphor, allusion, simile, theme, symbolism, irony, inference, prediction

Thinking
    Analysis, research

Vocabulary
    Target words, definition, application

Writing
    Essay, poetry, letter, eulogy, newspaper article

Listening/Speaking
    Discussion, interview, oral presentation, audio/video presentation, picture essay

Across the Curriculum
    Art—collage, caricature; Drama—script, charades; Current Events—articles, pictures; Music—appropriate selections

Genre: memoir

Setting: Coalwood, West Virginia, and surrounding communities; 1957–1960

Point of View: first-person

Themes: perseverance, relationships (family and interpersonal), nonconformity, destiny, motivation

Conflict: family, e.g., sibling rivalry, father-son; vocational

Tone: candid, conversational

Mood: optimistic

Style: narrative

Summary

Inspired by the 1957 launching of the Russian space satellite *Sputnik*, Homer Hickam, Jr. (Sonny), the 14-year-old son of a coal-mining superintendent in Coalwood, West Virginia, pursues his dream to build rockets and send them into space. If Sonny and the motley members of his rocket club succeed, they can leave Coalwood and seek academic careers rather than face uncertain futures in the mines of the slowly dying town. The boys persevere through numerous failures and the ridicule of those who believe they will never achieve their goal. They are spurred on by the faith of Sonny's mother, the boys' chemistry teacher, and other confident adults. Their rockets begin to illuminate the skies above Coalwood, and their dream brings hope to the town and surrounding communities.

Characters

Members of the BCMA (Big Creek Missile Agency):

Homer "Sonny" Hickam, Jr.: teenage narrator; resolutely follows his dream to build rockets and move away from Coalwood

Roy Lee: good-looking teenage boy; has own car; popular with girls

O'Dell: small, excitable teenage boy

Sherman: compact, muscular teenage boy; left leg shriveled and weak because of polio

Quentin: school "nerd;" intelligent; chosen to join the BCMA after initial rocket failures because Sonny believes he might know how to build a rocket

Billy: the last to join the BCMA; quick, intelligent

Homer Hickam, Sr.: Sonny's father; skeptical; mine superintendent; believes his younger son's future lies in the coal mines; favors his eldest son, Jim

Elsie (Lavender) Hickam: Sonny's mother; determined that he will escape the drudgery of life in the mines; has faith in his dream; dislikes her husband's attachment to the coal mines

Jim Hickam: Sonny's older brother; athletic; arrogant; primarily concerned about success of the football team

Freida Joy Riley: chemistry teacher; encourages Sonny

Isaac Bykovski: miner who uses his welding skills to assist Sonny; eventually dies in the mines

Mary Bykovski: Isaac Bykovski's wife; inspires Sonny to continue to build his rockets to honor her husband

Jake Mosby: junior mine engineer; encourages Sonny; instrumental in getting news of rockets publicized

John Dubonnet: leader of the union; conflicts with Homer, Sr.; encourages Sonny's dream

Geneva Eggers: prostitute in Coalwood; as a child, she was saved from a fire by Homer Hickam, Sr.; saves Sonny from freezing to death in the snow

Dorothy Plunk: beautiful; Sonny's "dream girl" who just wants to be his friend

Emily Sue Buckleberry: Dorothy's best friend; Sonny's confidante

Valentine: teenage girl who consoles Sonny

Rev. "Little" Richard: minister for black congregation

Rev. Josiah Lanier: Methodist preacher for company church

R. L. Turner: high school principal whose skepticism turns to enthusiasm

Mr. Hartsfield: math teacher

Dr. Wernher von Braun: German rocket scientist who does not appear personally but whose research inspires Sonny and Quentin

Clinton Caton: welder; key person in Sonny's win at National Science Fair

Mr. Fuller: temporary superintendent of Coalwood; tries unsuccessfully to stop the BCMA's rocket launches

Background Information

Sputnik: the name of a series of unmanned satellites launched by the Soviet Union

October 4, 1957: *Sputnik 1;* first artificial Earth satellite; circled the earth once every 96 minutes at a speed of 18,000 mph; fell to earth January 4, 1958. The Soviet Union launched nine larger *Sputnik* satellites between November 1957 and March 1961.

National Aeronautics and Space Administration (NASA): established 1958

Explorer 1: first United States satellite; launched January 31, 1958

United Mine Workers of America (UMWA): an industrial trade union that represents mine workers in many coal mines and coal-processing industries in the United States. The union organized miners in its first location in West Virginia in 1902. John L. Lewis served as president from 1920 until his retirement in 1960.

Additional Information

The memoir was first published as *Rocket Boys: A Memoir* (Delacorte Press, 1998) and has since been translated into eight languages. Honors: one of *New York Times* Great Books of 1998; alternate "Book-of-the-Month" selection for the Literary Guild and the Doubleday book clubs; nominated by National Book Critics Circle as Best Biography of 1998. Universal Studios released the film version of the book, *October Sky*, in 1999, and the book was re-titled and mass released as a paperback edition. As *October Sky*, the book reached #1 on the *New York Times* bestseller list. Note that *October Sky* is an anagram for *Rocket Boys*.

About the Author

Personal: Homer H. Hickam, Jr. was born February 19, 1943, to Homer, Sr., and Elsie (Lavender) Hickam. He and his older brother Jim grew up in Coalwood, West Virginia, where their father was superintendent of the local coal mine. He and his wife Linda, live in Huntsville, Alabama, "Rocket City, USA."

Education: Hickam graduated from Big Creek High School in 1960 and received a BS degree in Industrial Engineering from Virginia Polytechnic Institute in 1964.

Military: He served in the U.S. Army for six years. He received the Army commendation and Bronze Star medals for his duty as a First Lieutenant, Fourth Infantry Division, in Vietnam, 1967–1968. After six years of active duty, he left the Army with the rank of Captain.

Career: From 1971–1981, Hickam was employed as an engineer for the U.S. Army Missile command, working in Huntsville, Alabama, and Germany. In 1981 he began his career with NASA as an aerospace engineer at Marshall Space Flight Center. During his tenure with NASA, he trained astronauts for various types of missions, including the Hubble Space Telescope mission. He retired from NASA in 1998.

Literary Career: His first book, *Torpedo Junction* (1989), was followed by *Rocket Boys: A Memoir* (1998); his first fiction novel, *Back to the Moon* (1999); two more memoirs, *The Coalwood Way* (2000) and *Sky of Stone: A Memoir* (2001); and a self-help/inspiration book, *We Are Not Afraid: Strength and Courage from the Town That Inspired the #1 Bestseller and Award-winning Movie* October Sky (2002). *The Keeper's Son* also became available October 2003.

Patterns for Poems

Diamente (contrast): Line 1—one word (noun, subject); Line 2—two words (adjectives describing line 1); Line 3—three words ("-ing" or "-ed" words that relate to line 1); Line 4—four words (first two words relate to line 1; second two nouns relate to line 7); Line 5—three words ("-ing" or "-ed" words that relate to line 7; Line 6—two words (adjectives describing line 7); Line 7—one word (noun that is opposite of line 1)

Five-Senses (describing an emotion): Line 1—color of the emotion; Line 2—sound of the emotion; Line 3—taste of the emotion; Line 4—smell of the emotion; Line 5—sight (what the emotion looks like); Line 6—feeling evoked by the emotion. Each line can be a phrase or a sentence.

Limerick: a five-line nonsense poem, written in anapestic lines. An anapest is a metrical foot of three syllables, with two unaccented syllables followed by an accented one. The first, second, and fifth lines rhyme and consist of three feet. The third and fourth lines rhyme and consist of two feet.

Initiating Activities

1. Ask students if they have heard of the book or the movie. Have them preview the book, noting the title, dedication, cover illustration, Author's Note, and teasers on the book cover, and then make predictions about the book.

2. Place the term "perseverance" on an overhead transparency. Brainstorm with students: definition, synonyms, antonyms, personal examples.

3. Place the phrase, "parental expectations vs. an adolescent's personal dreams" on an overhead transparency. Brainstorm with students: personal examples, probable conflict, possibility of resolution.

4. Read aloud, "You see things; and you say, 'Why?' but I dream things that never were; and I say, 'Why not?'" (George Bernard Shaw, *Back to Methuselah,* Pt. I, Act I, 1921). Brainstorm with students: those who only dream; those who dream and act; those who never dream. Present the name Homer Hickam, Jr. as one who dreams and acts.

5. Read aloud the quotes from Dr. Wernher von Braun and Miss Freida Joy Riley found at the beginning of the book. Elicit students' responses as to whether they agree or disagree with the quotations and why.

Cause/Effect

Directions: To plot cause and effect in a story, first list the sequence of events. Then mark causes with a C and effects with an E. Sometimes in a chain of events, one item may be both a cause and an effect. Draw arrows from cause statements to the appropriate effects.

Events in the story	Cause	Effect
1.		
2.		
3.		
4.		
5.		
6.		
7.		
8.		
9.		
10.		

Another way to map cause and effect is to look for an effect and then backtrack to the single or multiple causes.

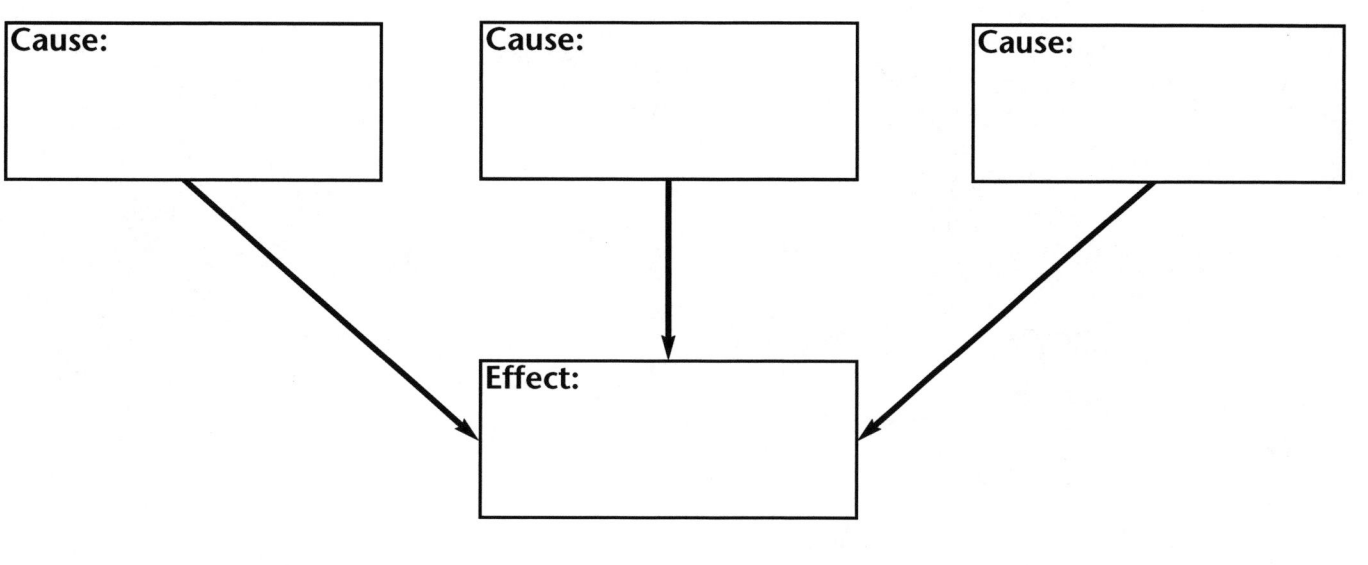

Sociogram

Directions: Write the name of a different character in each circle. On the "spokes" surrounding each character's name, write several adjectives that describe that character. On the arrows joining one character to another, write a description of the relationship between the two characters. How does one character influence the other?

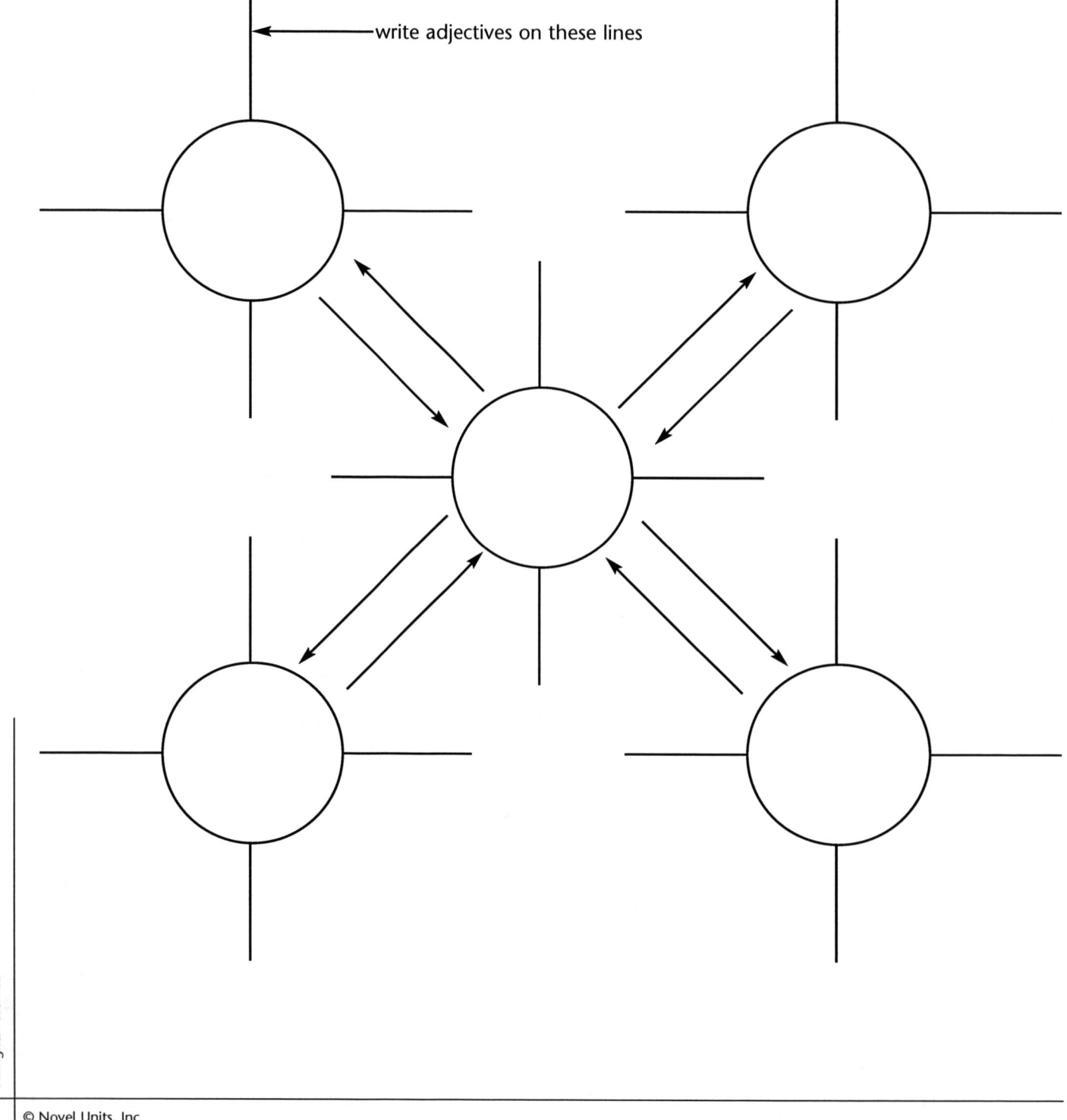

Attribute Web

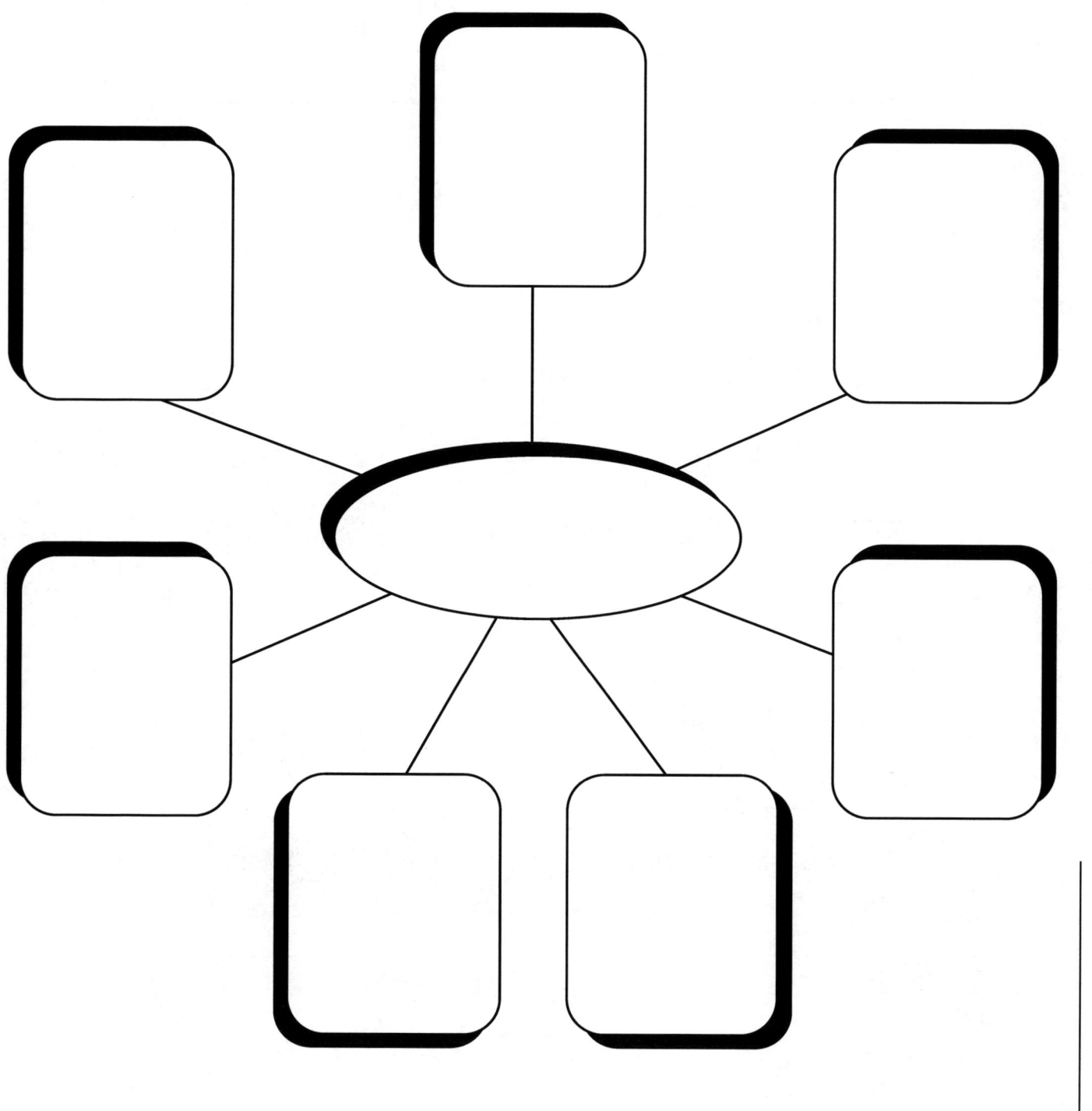

Story Map

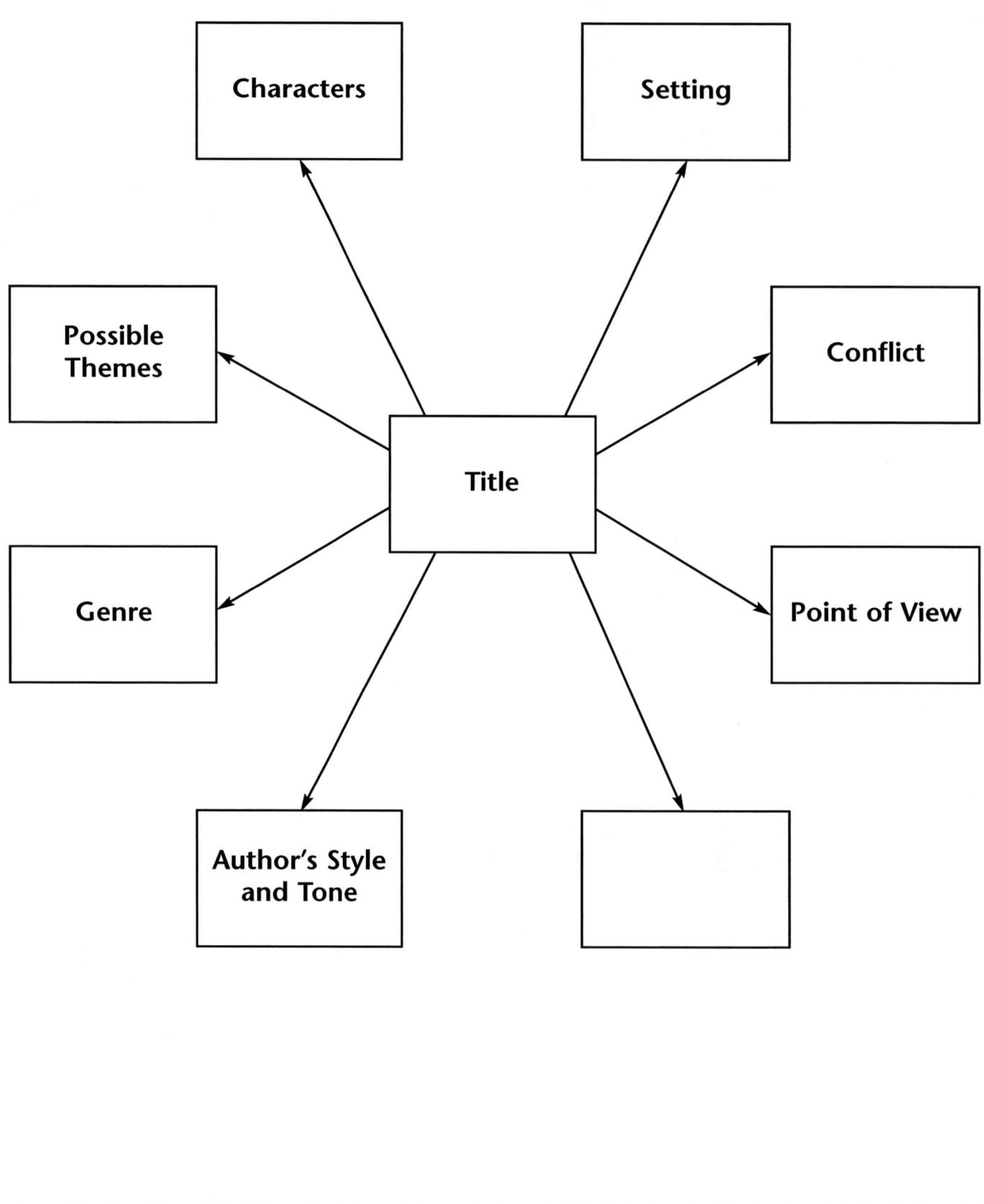

Understanding Values

Values represent people's beliefs about what is important, good, or worthwhile. For example, most families value spending time together.

Directions: Think about the following characters from *October Sky* and the values they exhibit: Sonny Hickam, Homer Hickam, Sr., Elsie Hickam, Jim Hickam, Dorothy Plunk, Miss Riley. What do they value? What beliefs do they have about what is important, good, or worthwhile? On the chart below, list each character's three most important values, from most important to least. Be prepared to share your lists during a class discussion.

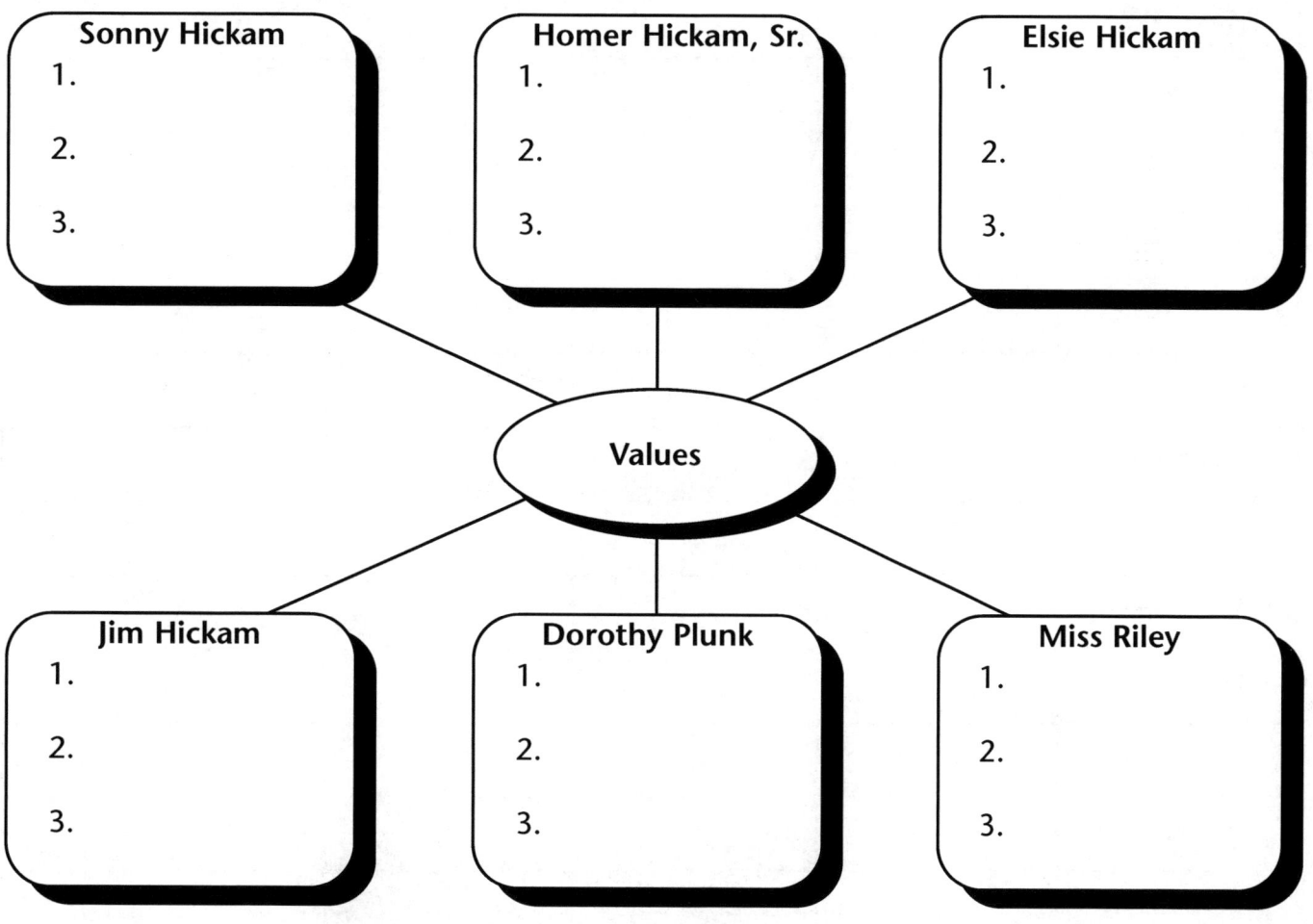

After you have finished the chart and participated in the class discussion, think about which character seems to have values most like your own. Write a paragraph that explains why you chose this character.

Rocket Chart

Rocket	Type	Results	Problems	Modifications
#1				
#2				
Auk I				
Auks II–IV				
Auks V–VIII				
Auks IX–XI				
Auks XII–XIII				
Auks XIV–XV				
Auks XVI–XIX				
Auk XX				
Auk XXI				
Auk XXII–A				
Auk XXII–B				
Auk XXII–C				
Auk XXII–D				
Auk XXIII				
Auk XXIV				
Auk XXV				
Auks XXVI–XXXI				

Note: Examples of literary devices found in each section are included in the Supplementary Activities when applicable. Guide students to identify these devices as they read the book. For clarification in the discussion questions, Homer "Sonny" Hickam, Jr. is referred to as Sonny and his father as Homer.

Chapter 1, pp. 1–16

Homer "Sonny" Hickam, Jr. tells about his life in his hometown of Coalwood, West Virginia, in 1957. Although Sonny is apparently destined to become a coal miner like his father, his mother emphasizes that he is not just like his father.

Vocabulary
enthalpy (1)
kinetic (1)
bituminous coal (1)
sonorous (4)
pristine (7)
tipple (11)

Discussion Questions

1. Discuss Coalwood, West Virginia, and how Sonny's family reacts to their life there. Elicit students' responses concerning the author's chance of leaving Coalwood and achieving a better life. *(Almost everyone in Coalwood works for the company that owns the coal mine, and every Coalwood family must have a father who works for the company. The company owns the miners' houses, the church, the hotel, and the store; it also pays the salary for the doctor, dentist, and minister of the main church. The company's general superintendent's mansion sits on a hill overlooking the town. Main Street leads to the cluster of miners' houses. When it forks to the "colored" camps, the pavement ends. Sonny's parents, Homer, Sr. and Elsie, disagree about how he and his older brother, Jim, will live their lives. Homer is the mine superintendent and believes Sonny is destined to live and work in Coalwood. Sonny's mother tells him he is not just like his father. Sonny is proud to live in Coalwood. pp. 1–3, 15–16; Responses will vary.)*

2. Analyze Elsie Hickam's feelings about life in Coalwood. Analyze the significance of her mural and the metaphor comparing the Olga Coal Company to a mistress. *(She hauls in dirt and plants a rose garden, attempting to find color in the black/gray atmosphere of the coal-mining town. Mural: Since Homer became the mine superintendent, she has been painting a mural of a seashore. The mural symbolizes Elsie's dream of a reality different from her life in Coalwood. Metaphor: Elsie feels threatened by Homer's time-consuming loyalty to the mine as if he were spending the time with a mistress. pp. 2, 14–15)*

3. Discuss George L. Carter and William Laird and why they are important to the story. *(Carter founded Coalwood. When his son came home from WWI, he brought Laird with him. Carter hired Laird to be in charge of operations at the mine. Laird established peace, prosperity, and tranquility for the citizens of Coalwood. He cared not only about the company but also about the miners and their families. He improved their living conditions and established programs such as Boy and Girl Scouts. His improvements in mining operations included concerns for the miners' safety. Because of his legacy, Coalwood was spared much of the violence, poverty, and pain of other coal-mining towns. The people of Coalwood refer to Laird as "Captain" because of their respect for him. It was the Captain who gave Homer Hickam the opportunity to become superintendent of the mine. pp. 6–9)*

4. Discuss Homer Hickam, Sr. Examine his relationship with his family, particularly Sonny. Analyze the ramifications of a "workaholic" parent. *(He started working for the Carter mine as a common miner when he was 22 years old. Because of his intelligence and effort, he became the Captain's protégé, rising to foreman and eventually becoming superintendent when the Captain retired. He asked Elsie to marry him after he became foreman. Because of Homer's dedication to the*

Captain and the mine, his family sees little of him. Sonny longs for his father's time and his touch. pp. 8–11; Responses will vary.)

5. Discuss Sonny's childhood and analyze how this impacted his life. Elicit students' responses concerning the impact of events of their childhood on their lives today. *(Sonny and his friends pretended to be miners, experiencing the unsettling effects of disappearing into the earth. The boys played around the railroad tracks, sometimes jumping into coal-filled cars. Sonny spent hours reading and developed a love for adventure and science fiction, but at his teachers' insistence, also developed diversity in his reading. He loved to read about real-life heroes who had courage and intelligence. Sonny couldn't see his life beyond Coalwood, yet dreams of adventure were planted in his mind. Sonny may not have known about his own future, but he did know his mother did not want him to become a miner. pp. 11–14; Responses will vary.)*

Supplementary Activities

1. Have students (a) identify the profession of one of their parents and explain briefly why they do or do not plan to follow that parent's footsteps or (b) identify and explain briefly a time they were part of a childhood group or club similar to the Coalhicans. Their responses can be oral or written.

2. Note the allusion to the Depression. Have students ask grandparents or other senior citizens about their memories of the Depression, then participate in an oral discussion.

Chapter 2, pp. 17–44

News of the Russian space satellite *Sputnik* changes Sonny's life. Sonny is intrigued by stories of Dr. Wernher von Braun and his work at Cape Canaveral. Sonny, Roy Lee, O'Dell, and Sherman build and launch their first rocket. Sonny and Jim experience intense sibling rivalry.

Vocabulary

precipitously (26)
prowess (33)
proclivity (33)
inexorable (39)
molecule (39)

Discussion Questions

1. Examine the universality of Sonny's feeling that he may be responsible for tension between his parents. *(Sonny knows that Jim blames him for the tension. Homer wanted a daughter and proclaimed his disappointment when Sonny was born. Elsie retaliated by naming the baby "Homer Hadley Hickam, Junior." The arguments between Homer and Elsie continue, and Sonny feels their discontent has left him with a heavy name. Note that it is not uncommon for children to blame themselves for tension between parents, especially if they hear their names mentioned in an argument. p. 17)*

2. Discuss why Sonny divides his life into two distinct phases. *(He sees his life as pre-Sputnik and post-Sputnik. After Sputnik is launched October 5, 1957, changes occur in the community, the school, and in Sonny's personal life. Community: almost every word on the radio is about Sputnik. A radio disk jockey cautions students they must "catch up with the Russians." Newspapers carry articles about American scientists and engineers at Cape Canaveral and their desperate attempts to catch up with Russia. School: The Student Council responds to the threat of Sputnik with a resolution dedicating the rest of the year to academic excellence. Student conversations depict their apprehension and misconceptions of the Russians. Sonny: becomes intrigued by stories of Dr. Wernher von Braun and begins to picture himself away from Coalwood, working with von Braun. He ultimately announces his plans to build a rocket to Roy Lee, O'Dell, and Sherman. They attempt to launch their first rocket. Note that Sputnik is a pivotal point in Sonny's life. Throughout chapter)*

3. Contrast Jim and Sonny Hickam and analyze Sonny's statement, "...I was raised an only child and so was my brother" (p. 21). Analyze their "truce." Examine whether or not Homer's apparent favoritism for Jim is intentional. Elicit students' responses concerning emotions created by favoritism and the impact of hurtful words. *(The boys are quite different, and this causes them to have little to do with each other. Jim is older and is the best-dressed boy in school. He is the "pride" of his father, who often brags about his skills on the football field. Sonny is smaller, near-sighted, unconcerned about how he looks, has no interest in football, and plays in the band. The rivalry between the brothers leads to an intense fight that leaves them both injured and frightened, causing them to enter an uneasy truce. pp. 21-23, 33-35; Responses will vary.)*

4. Examine the resentment directed toward Sonny at school and correlate this with his friendship with O'Dell, Sherman, and Roy Lee. Examine the boys' importance to Sonny. *(Other boys in school resent Sonny for being the son of the mine superintendent and often seek revenge against him. This resentment stems from their fathers, who feel that Homer is "uppity" because he has achieved his position in spite of not having a college degree. The other three boys feel no resentment and remain Sonny's loyal friends throughout the years. They are the ones to whom he turns when he wants to build a rocket because he trusts them and knows they are true friends. pp. 24-27)*

5. Discuss Big Creek High School and its initial importance to Sonny. *(The school is a grimy three-story building on the outskirts of War, a run-down community. The football field is carefully tended, indicating the importance of football to the community. The football boys have their choice of girls. Until Sputnik, academics took second place to athletics. A train track near the school, with its rumble of coal cars, is a constant reminder of the importance of the mine. Sonny struggles with algebra and is more interested in Dorothy Plunk than in academics. pp. 27-30)*

6. Discuss Roy Lee's and Jim's preoccupation with girls. *(Roy Lee is more interested in girls than in anything else. He repeatedly gives Sonny advice about how to gain Dorothy's affection. He entices Sonny with stories about the "backseat of the car." Roy Lee decides he must go out for football so girls will react to him as they do to Jim. Girls are drawn to Jim, and he enjoys the attention. p. 38; Throughout book)*

7. Examine the beginnings of Sonny's desire to build a rocket. Analyze the reactions of other people. *(He is inspired when he reads about and sees drawings of rockets in* Newsweek *and* Life. *He remembers reading that von Braun built rockets in his youth. He announces his plans to build a rocket. Homer: says nothing; Sonny doubts he heard him. Elsie: "Don't blow yourself up." Roy Lee: "Where? All right, let's do it!" O'Dell: "What material?" Sherman: "How?" Note the enthusiasm of Roy Lee and the practicality of O'Dell and Sherman. pp. 41-42)*

8. Discuss the design of the first rocket and the results of the launch. Note the teamwork of the boys. *(Design: small plastic flashlight with hole in the base for the body; powder from cherry bombs placed in flashlight and wrapped in electrical tape; fuse from cherry bomb; apparatus glued to inside fuselage of plastic model airplane. Launch: from top of fence in Elsie's rose garden; Sherman gives the countdown, Roy Lee carries the matches, O'Dell lights the match and hands it to Sonny, who lights the fuse and runs. Result: huge black flash, arc of fire in sky, blows up fence. pp. 42-44)*

9. **Prediction:** What consequences will Sonny face after the rocket fiasco?

Supplementary Activities

1. Have students interview someone who remembers *Sputnik*, and ask him/her about individual and community reaction to the satellites. Students should present oral, audio, or video presentations to the class.

2. Working in small groups (a) have students write a five-senses poem reflecting their emotions when someone made them feel inadequate in sports, music, academics, etc. or (b) create a "rocket" patterned after Sonny's design, using sand instead of cherry bomb powder.

3. Literary devices: **Similes**—von Braun was "like Michelangelo…Lewis and Clark;" (Elsie's smile) "like a hundred-watt bulb" (p. 36); I stared at it *(Sputnik)*…as "if it had been God Himself in a golden chariot" (p. 38) **Metaphors**—Franklin Delano Roosevelt: Antichrist, Harry Truman: vice-Antichrist, John L. Lewis: Lucifer (p. 19); Dorothy Plunk: "God's perfection" (p. 31)

Chapters 3–4, pp. 45–70

Sonny faces the consequences of the failed rocket. His mother encourages him to build another one. Sonny experiences inner conflict over his dad's favoritism for Jim. The national recession begins to affect the economy in Coalwood. Tension arises between Homer and the mine union members. Homer, after being ill for quite awhile, sees a doctor and is told he has a "spot" on his lung.

Vocabulary
impotent (55)
entity (62)
surreptitiously (65)

Discussion Questions

1. Examine the immediate effects of the boys' first rocket "launch." Elicit students' responses as to how their parents would have reacted had they launched a rocket with this result. *(Immediate: A big chunk of the fence arcs into the sky; burning debris falls; a thunderous echo resounds from surrounding hollow; dogs bark; house lights come on and people huddle on front porches, wondering if the mine has blown up or Russians are attacking; Elsie reacts in disbelief; Homer is uninterested; Sonny's friends run away. pp. 45–46; Responses will vary.)*

2. Analyze the argument between Homer and Elsie following Sonny's rocket fiasco. Discuss how their conflicts always seem to turn toward the mine. Why do you think Elsie is so upset that Homer continues to work in the mine? *(Homer tells Elsie to take care of Sonny before he embarrasses him all over Coalwood. Elsie responds sarcastically that maybe Homer's mine workers will refuse to work for him as a result of Sonny's failure. They begin their standard quarrel about the mine. Homer reminds Elsie that the mine provides for her and the boys; she responds that the mine is a death trap. pp. 47–48; Responses will vary.)*

3. Examine the conversation between Sonny and his mother after the failed rocket and what this reveals about both of them. *(In response to her question, "Do you think you could build a real rocket?" Sonny replies, "No, ma'am, I don't know how." Elsie tells him she is concerned about his future, and it is time he quit drifting along, playing games, and instigating wild schemes. She tells him his dad thinks the best he can do is work at the mine. Sonny questions her about why his dad doesn't like him. She replies it isn't that Homer doesn't like Sonny, but he is too busy with the mine to think about him. Elsie knows Coalwood is going to die, and Sonny must find a way to go to college. Elsie: thinks Sonny can build a rocket and wants him to prove it to his father; is concerned about her son and his future; tries to shield Sonny from Homer's indifference. Sonny: longs for his father's approval; feels inadequate. pp. 49–52)*

4. Analyze the teasing, tormenting, and harassment following the rocket failure and the effect on those involved. *(Buck Trant taunts the "rocket boys," calling them "Little idiot moron sisters." Roy Lee, O'Dell, and Sherman bow their heads in helpless rage. Sonny retaliates with an insulting remark about Buck's mother. Both Sonny and Buck are put off the bus. The other three later tell Sonny they're not going to build another rocket. Jim tells Sonny he is a complete moron, and everybody is laughing at the family because of him. Pooky Suggs calls Sonny "Homer's little rocket boy" and blames Sonny and Homer for his father's death inside the mine. Effect: A miner defends Sonny against Pooky, and other miners encourage him by calling him "Rocket Boy." Sonny is determined to build another rocket. pp. 55–60)*

5. Discuss Homer's interference in the football team's concerns. Analyze what this reveals about Homer. *(The football team wins all its games, but is declared ineligible to play in the state championship game. Homer, as president of the Football Fathers, intervenes by getting a lawyer to file a lawsuit. The case is thrown out on a technicality, and the Big Creek High School football team's season is officially over. Jim is furious. Homer vows to file an appeal, resisting Elsie's attempts to dissuade him. Homer's conduct shows his determination to give Jim a chance at a football scholarship and reveals his stubbornness and self-assurance. pp. 60–63)*

6. Examine the union/management conflict in Coalwood. Compare this with news stories about present-day strikes. *(After WWII, Coalwood became a more profitable mine operation, thus ending 50 years of labor peace. Mr. Carter resisted the efforts of the United Mine Workers of America [UMWA] to organize a union in Coalwood. The union ordered a strike, and Carter ordered the mines to be closed. President Truman sent U.S. Navy personnel to reopen the mines, and Carter eventually was forced to sign a contract with the union. He sold Coalwood. The Captain and Homer Hickam stayed. An edgy peace, with intermittent strikes, marked the next decade. By 1957, most of the old union leaders had retired, and the new ones wanted to show their worth. John Dubonnet, a classmate of Homer and Elsie, is now the union leader. A national recession forces Homer to lay off some miners, and the union local threatens to strike. Dubonnet and Homer engage in a bitter verbal conflict, each accusing the other of various transgressions and inadequacies, ranging from personal to business. They part with nothing settled. Elsie is caught in the middle because of Homer's and her former friendship with Dubonnet. His parting words taunt Homer, "Elsie, you're a fine woman. I always thought you deserved better." pp. 64–68; Responses and comparisons will vary.)*

7. **Prediction:** How will Homer's illness affect him and his family?

8. **Prediction:** Will the union/management conflict lead to violence?

Supplementary Activities

1. Begin a classroom chart using the Rocket Chart on page 12 of this guide. Add information for the first rocket to the chart. This is a continuing activity throughout the book.
Note: See Post-reading Discussion Question #5 on page 34 of this guide for an example of the completed chart.

2. Have students research John L. Lewis and the UMWA and participate in an oral discussion.

3. Literary Devices: **Similes**—O'Dell's eyes were "as wide as the barn owls" (p. 45); "Coalwood's going to die deader than a hammer" (p. 51) **Metaphors**—coal mine: death trap (p. 47); sound of coal cars, locomotives, and miners: Coalwood's industrial symphony (p. 53) **Allusions**—"And if the blind leadeth the blind, both shall fall into the ditch," Bible, Luke 6:39 (p. 61); Iwo Jima (p. 63)

Chapter 5, pp. 71–87

Quentin, the school "nerd," joins Sonny's rocket-building group. Sonny, Quentin, and Roy Lee have two more failed attempts at flying a rocket. Sonny finds the courage to ask Dorothy Plunk out on a date.

Vocabulary

oxidizer (74)
succinctly (77)
insidious (78)
cohesiveness (78)
saltpeter (79)
casement (83)

Discussion Questions

1. Analyze the interaction between Quentin and Sonny, noting Quentin's response to Sonny and Sonny's reaction to Quentin. Elicit students' responses: Who uses whom to get what he wants? *(Quentin is the class nerd. He uses big words, carries an overstuffed briefcase, and reads while others participate in sports. He seems to have no friends, always eats alone, and people make fun of him. Sonny thinks Quentin is a genius because he gets excellent grades in all subjects. Sonny approaches Quentin because he thinks he might know how to build a rocket. Quentin: suspicious; thinks Sonny wants to copy his homework; says he is not surprised Sonny has come to him. He agrees to help because he thinks Sonny has leadership abilities he lacks and can get all the materials he needs. Quentin hopes to promote his goal of working at Cape Canaveral some day. Sonny: irritated, but fascinated with Quentin; is reluctant to be associated with him; doesn't want football players to see them shaking hands. pp. 71–75; Responses will vary.)*

2. Play a recording of "Sixteen Tons" or distribute a copy of the song's lyrics to students. Compare/contrast the Coalwood company store with the stereotype in the song. *(Coalwood: source of town's cohesiveness, contains a little bit of everything, has fair prices and a college-educated manager who watches credit closely to prevent miners from growing too deeply in debt. Stereotype: credit too easy; inflated prices; miners too deeply in debt are paid with scrip, which is only good in the company store. pp. 77–78)*

3. Examine the steps Sonny takes to prepare for his second rocket launch, the reaction of others, and the results. Discuss why Quentin is important to Sonny. *(According to Quentin's instructions, Sonny purchases saltpeter from the company store. The two boys experiment with the powder in Sonny's basement "rocket laboratory" and put the two best mixtures in aluminum tubing casements, place a broom handle in one end, and make cardboard fins. Reactions: Junior, at the store, cautions that Sonny could blow himself up. Dubonnet: tells Sonny he is too smart to stay in Coalwood and wishes him good luck. Quentin: views their experiment as a basis for modification and records results in "Body of Knowledge" journal. Roy Lee: appears to watch. Importance of Quentin to Sonny: makes him feel scientific no matter what happens; without his encouragement, Sonny might have been embarrassed to fail, but now he feels failure will add to their knowledge. Results: first rocket emits a terrible smell and falls over; glue on fins melts [too weak]; second rocket blows up [too strong]. Homer reminds Sonny he has told him not to do this again and wants him to stop. Elsie again acts as the buffer, telling Sonny just to do it in another place. pp. 79–85)*

4. Discuss Sonny and Dorothy's "date" at her house. Contrast Sonny's reasons for being there with Dorothy's reasons for having him there. *(Instead of studying biology as planned, Sonny and Dorothy talk about all sorts of things other than school. Dorothy asks Sonny many questions about himself, his family, and his experiences. Sonny is pleased to be with Dorothy, no matter what they talk about. Dorothy seems only interested in being friends with Sonny and about the interesting things he has done. She is not attracted to Sonny and avoids his invitation for another date. pp. 85–87)*

Supplementary Activities
1. Add information for the second rocket to the Rocket Chart.
2. Have students draw a caricature of Quentin or write a limerick about him based on his description on page 72 of the novel.
3. Literary Devices: **Metaphor**—line of miners: "river of black, bobbing helmets" (p. 81) **Universality**—teenage boys' interest in sex, e.g., Quentin's comments about *Tropic of Cancer*, Roy Lee's suggestion of "parking"

Chapters 6–7, pp. 88–128

Sonny forms the Big Creek Missile Agency (BCMA). Isaac Bykovski assists the boys in building their rockets. One of the rockets lands close to the mine, and Homer forbids Sonny to launch more rockets. Elsie and the Great Six (elementary school teachers) intervene on the Rocket Boys' behalf. Homer finally relents, showing Sonny a deserted field outside of Coalwood where the boys can launch their rockets.

Vocabulary
nefarious (94)
propellant (98)
prodigious (100)
pernicious (104)
cupidity (105)
cogitative (106)
subjective (119)
rabble-rouser (121)
petulance (124)

Discussion Questions
1. Examine the interaction between Homer and Sonny after the Army Ballistic Missile Agency's (ABMA) rocket launch. *(Sonny and his friends are elated after watching the successful rocket launch on TV. Homer comes downstairs and asks if it worked. Sonny tells his dad, "We're going into space," and his dad replies, "Little man... I think sometimes you're already there." Sonny takes his remark as a compliment. This conversation marks the first time Homer and Sonny have had a meaningful interaction about rocketry and one of the few times Sonny has ever felt affirmed by his father. pp. 88–91)*

2. Discuss the formation of the Big Creek Missile Agency (BCMA) and its significance. *(In imitation of von Braun's ABMA, Sonny decides to form his own missile agency and Roy Lee, O'Dell, Sherman, and Quentin join him. Their goal is to learn all about rockets and build them. Sonny is president, O'Dell is treasurer and in charge of supplies, Roy Lee will handle transportation, Sherman is in charge of publicity and setting up the rocket range, and Quentin is the agency's scientist. Significance: Sonny's goal is no longer to get a rocket into the air, but to learn about rockets and build them according to scientific specifications. The organization gives each boy a specific job, thus becoming more efficient and goal-oriented. pp. 90–91)*

3. Read aloud the quote from George Bernard Shaw's *Back to Methuselah* (see Initiating Activity #4) and correlate this with Quentin's opinion about the BCMA. Analyze the reactions of Jim and the other football players, Mr. Turner, and Miss Riley to Quentin and Sonny. *(Walking past the high school trophy case, Quentin remarks that one day the BCMA will have a trophy for their rockets. He assures Sonny he believes their rockets could be winners at the national science fair. [Note foreshadowing of the science fair trophy.] Reactions: Buck and other football players call them morons, tell them not to get their filthy handprints on the trophy case, and taunt and threaten them. Mr. Turner's dubious response to Quentin's dream of a science trophy is to tell the boys he will not tolerate a bomb in his school and that the football players don't need any help with their trophy case. Miss Riley thinks a science trophy is a wonderful idea and mentions the science fair. pp. 93–94)*

4. Examine Sonny's infatuation for Dorothy and Emily Sue's analysis of him. Elicit students' responses concerning the impact of teenage "love," especially when it is not reciprocated. *(Sonny and Dorothy study together on Sundays. Dorothy wants his friendship; he wants her love. Emily Sue, Sonny's "forever friend," catches his stares as Dorothy holds hands with a senior football player and tells him Dorothy will never be more than his friend. Her analysis: Sonny is one of the nicest, friendliest boys in school. Everybody likes him because he likes himself. Dorothy likes Sonny as a friend but will look elsewhere for love. pp. 96–98; Responses will vary.)*

5. Examine Sonny and Quentin's efforts to develop a successful rocket and those who help them. *(They work through problems in finding a practical propellant and continue to explore the "why" and "how" of rockets. Isaac Bykovski agrees to teach Sonny to solder the aluminum rockets together, even though he knows he could get in trouble with Homer. He builds three rockets for the boys and, when the solder melts during the launch, he builds three more out of steel, welding them instead of soldering them together. He thinks Homer should be proud of what is going on in the welding shop and tells Sonny he should tell his father. pp. 98–107)*

6. Analyze the meaning of the name (Auk) chosen for the rockets. *(An auk is a diving sea bird found in arctic regions. It has short wings, webbed feet, a short tail, and legs [its "mode of travel"] so far back it stands like a penguin. It is perfectly adapted to its environment. Symbolically, the boys dream of building rockets with perfect proportions and the right propellant to launch into the space environment.)*

7. Analyze Homer's reaction to *Auk IV* and its ramifications. Contrast Sonny's and Mr. Bykovski's reactions to the incident. *(Sonny agrees to launch the rocket close to the mine because he doesn't think it will work. Homer and men from the Ohio steel mill observe the rocket launch. It "attacks" the coal company and takes a big chunk out of the brick wall of Homer's office. Homer is embarrassed and furious, tells Sonny he could have killed someone, and forbids him to make any more rockets. He accuses Sonny of being a thief and knows Bykovski helped him. Elsie tells Sonny he used Bykovski and should have thought of the consequences of his actions. As punishment, Homer reassigns Bykovski to the mine. Sonny is filled with shame and revulsion for getting Bykovski in trouble and thinks his dad "is the meanest man in this town." Bykovski defends Homer and accepts his punishment. He encourages Sonny and tells him to make the rockets fly and show his dad what he and Sonny did together. pp. 108–114)*

8. Discuss Reverend Lanier's sermon. Analyze why he spoke on the topic and its effect on the congregation. Elicit students' responses concerning whether they agree or disagree with Reverend Lanier's ideas about the father-son relationship. *(General topic: fathers/sons. He relates the story of a father who drives a nail in a door every time his son does bad things. After the son repents, the father removes the nails, but the holes are still there. At this point, Sonny feels guilty, and Homer is smug. The minister then switches his approach and speculates on how the father could have loved and supported his son instead. He suggests the possibility that the holes reflected the father's irritation rather than his love. He alludes to the trouble in Coalwood and reminds the congregation of the joy in having a child who longs to learn. He concludes with the admonition for sons to obey their fathers and for fathers to help their sons dream. He refers directly to the case of the Rocket Boys. Effect: The minister receives "Amens" from the "Great Six;" the rocket boys are pleased; the football boys furiously whisper; the parents are silent; Homer and Mr. Van Dyke look sour; Elsie and Mrs. Van Dyke smile angelically. After church, Homer takes Sonny to an abandoned slack dump, "gives" him the entire valley for his rocket project, and agrees to build a blockhouse with the stipulation that the rocket launching must stay out of sight and mind in Coalwood. pp. 123–126; Responses will vary.)*

9. **Prediction:** What effect will the construction of Cape Coalwood have on the BCMA? on the relationship between Homer and Sonny?

Supplementary Activities
1. Add *Auks I–IV* to the Rocket Chart.
2. As a class project, write a diamente poem contrasting *optimism* and *pessimism*. Discuss characters who are optimistic and those who are pessimistic about the success of the BCMA.
3. Literary Devices: **Similes**—football players disappeared "as if they got sucked up into the ceiling" (p. 94); rocket "dropped like a dead bird" (p. 107); "hair glowed like molten silver" (p. 123) **Allusion**—"Rendering to Caesar what was Caesar's," Bible, Matthew 22:21

Chapters 8–9, pp. 129–162

Big Creek High School's football team is suspended as a result of Homer's lawsuit. The BCMA begins construction of Cape Coalwood. A young engineer at the mine, Jake Mosby, becomes important to the BCMA. Homer continues to provide materials for the boys, though he pretends it's only by accident. Sonny and his friends successfully launch a rocket.

Vocabulary

ballistic missile (129)
debacle (136)
polyhedron (152)
ironic (162)

Discussion Questions
1. Correlate events at Cape Canaveral with events at Cape Coalwood. *(Canaveral: business booming, launching missiles successfully; still experiencing failures but making progress; remain optimistic even after Russians successfully launch* Sputnik III; *NASA established 1958. Coalwood: Sonny secures materials from mine carpentry and welding shops; learns to barter with townspeople for other items; boys build blockhouse and pour concrete for launch pad; raise their flag; launch* Auk V. *pp. 129–130, 137–141, 151–154)*

2. Examine the cause/effect of the football team's suspension. Apply the adage, "Pride goes before a fall" to the status of the football boys. *(Cause: Football Fathers file a lawsuit against athletic commission to allow Big Creek to play in the 1957 state championship game. Effects: [1] The football team is suspended for all games for 1958 season. [2] Jim blames Homer and vows he will never forgive him. [3] Buck is despondent, believing he will never get a football scholarship. [4] Roles reverse, i.e., football boys walk around sullenly. [5] People resent Homer for interfering. [6] Football boys' "supremacy" is deflated; rocket boys' inflated. pp. 131–136)*

3. Develop a cause/effect chart for the success of *Sputnik* on Big Creek High School. Use the Cause/Effect chart on page 7 of this guide. *(Cause: Sputnik. Effects: [1] concern that American students not as well-educated as Russian students [2] restructuring of curriculum, i.e., more challenging [3] concentrated classroom work with much more homework [4] pep talk for academics [5] cheerleaders lead school song for academics rather than football. pp. 130–134)*

4. Discuss Jake Mosby and his significance to the BCMA. Analyze whether or not he fits the stereotype of a playboy, i.e., a man, usually wealthy, whose chief interest is having a good time. Note his reaction to the launching of *Auk V*. *(He is a junior engineer who comes to Coalwood from the Ohio mill. His dad owns about 20% of the steel mill that owns Coalwood. Through his acquaintance with Sonny, he becomes interested in the rocket boys' project. He invites a reporter from a small newspaper to watch the launch of* Auk V, *who then favorably publicizes the BCMA. Jake invites the boys to view space through his telescope and gives Sonny his old trig book*

so he can learn to calculate how high the rockets go. Stereotype: drinks excessively, wealthy, flamboyant, flaunts his familiarity with girls, drives a Corvette. Reaction to Auk: throws himself to the ground, lights cigarette with trembling hands, takes a drink; triggers memories of being in Korean War. pp. 143–147, 153–155)

5. Discuss the launch of *Auk V* and examine how it differs from *Auks I–IV*. *(The boys use a bottle-tested formula for their propellant. Sherman posts a public notice about the launch at the Big Store and the post office. Mr. Dubonnet, Jake Mosby, Tom Musick, and news reporter Basil Oglethorpe come to view the launch. Auk V climbs 50 feet, then veers directly toward spectators. The boys realize they must allow the powder to dry completely before using it and learn how to make the rockets fly straight. The boys' spirits and enthusiasm begin to rise. pp. 153–156)*

6. Analyze the irony of Sonny's experience with Jake's telescope. Compare this with the irony of Sonny's life. Elicit students' responses concerning ironies they sense in their own lives. *(He can see into space clearly but can't focus the telescope close enough to see Coalwood. He can see stars a million light-years away, but he can't see the town in which the telescope is located. Sonny's life: He has a clear vision of his future in space, but his life in Coalwood seems to be a blur. p. 162; Responses will vary.)*

Supplementary Activities

1. Add *Auks V–VIII* to the Rocket Chart.
2. Have students read the poem, "Invictus," by William Ernest Henley. Conduct class discussion on how this poem relates to students' feelings about their own future.
3. Have students draw a caricature of Basil Oglethorpe based on his description on pages 153–154 of the novel.
4. Literary Devices: **Similes**—"miners walked around with their eyes lined like Cleopatra's" (p. 151); "stars spread out like diamonds on a vast blanket of black velvet" (p. 161)
   Allusions—Valley Forge, Pearl Harbor (p. 129); Carter's Little Liver Pills, i.e., a patented medicine popular during this era (p. 145); Lowell Thomas (p. 154)

Chapters 10–11, pp. 163–205

The BCMA boys realize the need to expand their mathematical skills. Miss Riley encourages Sonny. A growing audience watches the launching of the rockets. Homer takes Sonny into the mine for the first time.

Vocabulary
deductive (169)
infinity (169)
coalescing (170)
primordial (184)
viscous (186)
slurry (187)
theodolite (190)
methane (194)

Discussion Questions

1. Examine the conflict between the rocket boys and law enforcement. Discuss whether or not Van Dyke really intends to press charges or just wants to scare the boys. *(O'Dell and Roy Lee plan to take phones, presumably scrap, from the mule barn, which is mine property. They are trapped in the mule barn and get caught. Mr. Van Dyke confronts Sonny and the other boys with the "crime" of breaking and entering to commit theft, with a penalty of jail time. Van Dyke decides to extend "mercy" to the boys because Tag Farmer, the constable, considers them to be good boys. pp. 172–176; Responses will vary.)*

2. Examine why changes occur in the public's opinion of the BCMA boys, the boys' academic progress, and the boys' social status. *(The public becomes excited about their progress primarily because of publicity in the newspaper. Rocketry provides the incentive for Sonny to study hard, make good grades in plane geometry, and want to know about curves, angles, and polygons for rocket design. Sonny and Quentin begin to teach themselves trig from Jake's book. Social status: Some girls become more interested in the BCMA boys than in football boys. pp. 163–167)*

3. Discuss Miss Riley and her impact on the BCMA. Elicit students' responses concerning the attributes of an excellent teacher. *(She is the high school chemistry teacher. She is strict but has a sense of humor, is easy to talk to, and expresses interest in their rocketry. Her demonstration of rapid oxidation causes the BCMA boys to think of rocket fuel. Sonny tells her about the BCMA, and she repeats Elsie's plea, "Don't blow yourself up!" pp. 177–184; Responses will vary.)*

4. Discuss changes in the BCMA. Analyze Elsie's contributions to the BCMA and note the gradual changes in the relationship between Sonny and Homer. *(Billy joins the BCMA. He assists in the launches, beginning with Auk X. The boys experiment with saltpeter and sugar, eventually creating "rocket candy." They "borrow" equipment from Elsie's kitchen and Homer's garage. Elsie provides insight for draining fluid from the pot, offers advice about cleaning the pot, and continues to tell the boys not to blow themselves up. Throughout all their experiments, she never shames them for destroying her things and always believes they will succeed. Homer begins to express an interest in Sonny's work and asks about his latest experimentation with propellant and how effective it will be. Sonny is startled when his dad replies "Attaboy!" to Sonny's response to his question. pp. 181–189)*

5. Examine the events surrounding Sonny's trip into the mine. Analyze what this reveals about Sonny, Homer, and Elsie. *(When Homer learns of Sonny's desire to be an engineer, he wants him to see what he thinks a real engineer's job is. This marks a distinct change in Homer's relationship with Sonny, i.e., he asks Sonny, not Jim, to go into the mine with him. Without telling Elsie, Homer takes Sonny into the mine, where he explains engineering techniques necessary to safe mining. Sonny gains a new perspective and appreciation for his dad's work. Homer wants Sonny to become a mining engineer. Sonny senses Homer's love for the mine and is amazed that his dad shares such private thoughts with him. On their return to the surface, both Homer and Sonny face the "moment of truth," i.e., Sonny wants to become a space, not a mining, engineer. The closeness Sonny had felt to his dad in the mine disappears. Homer is disappointed with Sonny; Sonny blames himself for everything. Elsie, who is waiting for them when they emerge from the mine, is furious. She vows that the mine will not kill her sons as it is killing Homer. His response to her indicates that his love for the mine supercedes anything in his life. pp. 188–189, 193–205)*

Supplementary Activities

1. Add *Auks IX–XIII* to the Rocket Chart.

2. In small groups, have students create a collage depicting fear. Have each group give an oral presentation explaining the sources of fear depicted in their collage.

3. Read aloud Sonny's discovery on page 168 of the novel. "I had discovered that learning something, no matter how complex, wasn't hard when I had a reason to want to know it." Conduct class discussion, asking whether students agree or disagree with this idea. Have students cite examples that may prove this statement true, i.e., a 16-year old learning how to drive, a failing student athlete passing his/her classes to stay on the team, an actor memorizing his lines.

4. Literary Devices: **Similes**—(football boys) "like lost sheep" (p. 164); "steel casement was turned back like a banana peel" (p. 183); man-trip "squealed like a thousand tortured pigs;" mica "sparkled like diamonds" (p. 198); (coal dust) "like mother's milk" to Homer (p. 205) **Metaphor**—Coal: "life blood of this country" (p. 202)

Chapters 12–13, pp. 206–245

Leon Ferro assists the BCMA with welding. Miss Riley gives Sonny a book on missile design. Sonny faces danger in freezing cold weather and is rescued by Geneva Eggers.

Vocabulary

truncated (207)
tensile (213)
aperture (214)
parameters (217)

Discussion Questions

1. Discuss Elsie's reaction to Sonny's trip into the mine with his father. Elicit students' responses concerning their methods for dealing with an angry parent or guardian. *(She takes all her kitchen equipment from Sonny's lab. Sonny apologizes, and she "punishes" him by having him do chores around the house. Elsie eventually forgives Sonny and returns the equipment for his lab, but threatens more punishment if he ever enters the mine again. pp. 206–207; Responses will vary.)*

2. Analyze the "drawers" in Sonny's mind and how he deals with them. Elicit students' responses concerning "drawers" we close or keep open and why we do so. *(For the next several weeks, Homer retreats to the mine and isolates himself from Sonny. Sonny leaves this "drawer" closed until he knows what to say to his dad and has an opportunity to do so. The drawer concerning Mr. Bykovski remains open because Sonny knows he is responsible for Bykovski's return to the mine, and he is concerned that his allegiance to von Braun, a German, betrays Bykovski. He must have help to close this drawer, i.e., come to grips with his own guilt. He goes to the Bykovski home, where he apologizes to Mrs. Bykovski and discusses von Braun with Mr. Bykovski, who alludes to von Braun's role in the Holocaust and speaks of forgiveness and redemption. He allows Sonny to close this "drawer" by telling him it is okay to admire von Braun for what he has become and to forget what he had been. pp. 209–213; Responses will vary.)*

3. Examine what Sonny's request of Leon Ferro reveals about Sonny's maturation. Analyze how this event triggers positive results. *(Mr. Ferro agrees to do the welding for the rocket, but tells Sonny he must have an engineering drawing of the rocket. Sonny now believes he can do anything he wants to do if he works hard enough at it. Sonny draws the nozzle, then goes to his dad to ask his help, i.e., Ferro wants gravel delivered to his house in exchange for his welding. Homer asks to see Sonny's drawing and compliments him on his work. Sonny apologizes to his father about the day at the mine, and they once again begin to communicate. Although initially refusing to help Sonny, Homer supplies everything he requests. Men in the welding shop complete the work to Sonny's specifications and eventually produce work using some of their own ideas. pp. 213–219)*

4. Discuss the launches of *Auks XIV–XV*. *(Note that Auk XIV is the most successful rocket to date, soaring 3,000 feet into the air. Although Auk XV attains only half the altitude of Auk XIV, the boys gain knowledge each time they launch a rocket. pp. 217–220)*

5. Analyze the symbolism of Elsie's Christmas gift to Sonny and discuss reactions of others. *(She gives him a signed photograph of Dr. Wernher von Braun with a personal note in his own handwriting, ending with, "If you work hard enough, you will do anything you want." Sonny vows this is the most wonderful Christmas gift he has ever received. It symbolizes Sonny's ability to*

attain his dream of working with von Braun and his mother's faith in his ability to do so. He offers it to Jim and his father to read. Jim claims he doesn't know who von Braun is; Homer says he will read it but never does. Jim's reaction symbolizes the emotional distance between the two brothers; Homer's reaction symbolizes his mistrust of von Braun and his fear of losing Sonny to him. Quentin treats the photograph with awe and reverence, symbolizing the esteem with which he views von Braun and his work. p. 223)

6. Discuss Miss Riley's gift for Sonny and the effect it has on him. Analyze her statement, "All I've done is give you a book. You have to have the courage to learn what's inside it" (p. 232). *(She gives him a book,* Principles of Guided Missile Design. *He is elated that she has not forgotten their conversation about Sonny's attempts at rocket building. Her actions and words reveal her belief that Sonny can accomplish his dream, and she inspires him to believe he is ready for anything. He agrees to enter the science fair if Miss Riley wants him to. Her statement is the key point to learning. A book is only a tool, but the key is the courage to learn what is in the book. Sonny, or anyone, will learn only if he or she is willing to pursue knowledge and to dedicate the time and effort required for learning and applying the material. pp. 231–232)*

7. Discuss Sonny's experience in the freezing weather and what he learns about his dad as a result. *(He attempts to sled from Emily Sue's house but is only partially successful. He falls into deep snow and becomes wet and cold. He is afraid and realizes he can die in the freezing conditions that surround him. As he struggles to continue, Geneva Eggers appears and insists that he go home with her. She warms him up and feeds him. When she discovers he is Homer Hickam's son, she provides Sonny with some insight into his father, e.g., his taking care of everyone in the community where he grew up and his role in supporting his family when his father was injured. She asks Sonny to tell Homer of their meeting and of her help, but to tell him when his mother isn't listening. Homer later tells him Geneva's story. Homer rescued her from her house in Gary when it caught fire. The rest of her family, her parents and eight brothers, burned to death. Sonny learns from Homer that, after her husband's death, police from Gary chased her away, and Homer gave her a shack and told Tag to leave her alone. She is a prostitute and runs moonshine whiskey. Her story is to remain a secret between Homer and Sonny. Sonny feels strong pride for all his father has done. pp. 235–245)*

8. **Prediction:** Will Sonny's love for Dorothy ever be reciprocated?

9. **Prediction:** Will Sonny enter the science fair? If so, what will be the result?

Supplementary Activities

1. Add *Auks XIV–XV* to the Rocket Chart.

2. Have students conduct a poll in which they ask other students outside the class about the attributes of an excellent teacher. Divide into small groups to tally the results. Develop a classroom chart showing each attribute and the number of students who gave that response.

3. Literary Devices: **Similes**—(steps to putting a rocket together) like "putting stuff into different drawers in my mind" (p. 209); von Braun's photo and letter like "holy artifacts" (p. 223); (boys) walked in as if "we were kings of the earth" (p. 230) **Metaphors**—memory: drawers (p. 209); Roy Lee: greasy rat (p. 234) **Allusions**—Rockefellers (p. 207); Nazis (p. 211)

Chapters 14–16, pp. 246–273

The BCMA continues to learn through trial and error, and their rocket launches become increasingly more successful and widely acclaimed. The BCMA successfully refutes accusations of setting a forest fire with one of their rockets. Sonny convinces Principal Turner to offer a calculus class in school, but Sonny's grades aren't good enough to get him in the class. Tension between Sonny and his father continues.

Vocabulary

thermodynamics (248)
isentropic (248)
adiabatic (248)
elliptical (253)
trajectories (253)
overt (254)
ebullience (257)
flange (268)
guile (273)

Discussion Questions

1. Discuss the causes/effects of world-wide space exploration. Note how this affects the BCMA. *(Cause: Every time the United States launches a satellite, [Effect] the Russians launch one bigger and better. Cause: Russia attempts to reach the moon with the launching of Luna I. Effects: [1] Sonny unsuccessfully tries to locate the spacecraft with Jake's telescope and learns the next day that Luna I missed the moon. [2] Sonny mimics the U.S. politicians in his worry over whether or not the United States will catch up to the Russians in space, but he believes von Braun is doing something about it. [3] His concerns provide incentive to continue to learn as much as he can about rocket building. [4] He and Quentin realize the necessity of taking calculus and learning about differential equations in order to make correct calculations and to develop a De Laval nozzle. pp. 246–255)*

2. Examine types of conflict that are evident in this section and whether or not there is a resolution of each conflict. *(Russia vs. United States: space exploration; no resolution, pp. 246–247. Homer vs. Elsie: his inflexible determination to go into the mine when there is danger; ongoing conflict without resolution, pp. 250–251. Sonny and Quentin vs. Jim: Jim's jealousy over publicity the BCMA receives; boys leave but with no resolution, pp. 253–254. The BCMA vs. state troopers: suspicion that the BCMA's rocket started forest fire; resolved when Miss Riley points out the distance from rocket launch to fire is ten miles, an impossible distance for the BCMA's rocket, and Quentin proves an aeronautical flare started the fire, pp. 256–260. Sonny vs. Mr. Turner: Sonny is not allowed to take calculus because seven students sign up for a class that only accepts six, and Sonny's grades are the lowest of the seven; resolved when Quentin promises to teach Sonny, and Sonny resolves to teach himself from his father's self-study guide for mathematics, pp. 261, 264. Sonny vs. Homer: Sonny's continuing refusal to become a mining engineer; no resolution, pp. 266–267. Sonny vs. himself: doubts that he will ever know exactly who he is and what he is supposed to do; no resolution, p. 267. Sonny vs. Quentin: Sonny's impatience to perfect the rockets, Quentin's reluctance to hurry because of possibility of failure; uneasy resolution with Quentin feeling Sonny is changing too many things at once, pp. 269–271.)*

3. Add *Auks XVI–XX* to the Rocket Chart and discuss new discoveries the boys make about the rockets. Note the continuing change in public interest. *(The height attained by Auks XVI–XIX proves that, when going for altitude, bigger isn't always better. For the first time, several girls come to watch the launch of Auks XVI–XIX. Auk XX's blowout in the casement proves the need for seamless tubing. pp. 252–253, 271–272)*

4. Examine Mr. Hartsfield's negativity about forming a calculus class and the universality of his question, "Who ever told you boys life was fair?" Discuss why Mr. Turner allows the class to form and the impact one person can have on the "system." *(Mr. Hartsfield believes Quentin is the only one of the six boys in the BMCA capable of learning calculus. He does not believe Mr. Turner will authorize the class and sees no hope for it because Big Creek High School is, and always*

has been, a football and coal miner's school. When the boys and Miss Riley approach Mr. Turner about the class, he is initially sarcastic about the "pipe-bomb boy" and assures them the county superintendent will never approve it. pp. 256–261; Responses will vary.)

5. Analyze the dual irony of Sonny's not being allowed to take calculus. *(He is the BCMA boy who most vigorously campaigned for the class, but because seven students sign up for a six-student class, and his grades are the lowest of the seven, he does not get to join the class. Ironically, the student who prevents his joining the class is Dorothy Plunk, the "love of his life." p. 261)*

6. Discuss the changes in disposition of members of the Hickam family and why this occurs. *(Homer is in a frenzy because the demands on the mine are increasing. He recalls miners who had been cut-off the year before, and the company goes to an intense seven-day workweek. Elsie pensively continues to work on her mural, putting a house on the beach, reflecting her desire to escape from the mine's demands. Homer is elated when college football coaches arrive to offer Jim a scholarship, erasing his despondency of the past year. Sonny feels remote from the family and decides he must "open his own window" by teaching himself calculus from his father's guide for self-study. pp. 263–264)*

7. Analyze Sonny's dialogue with his father about Cape Coalwood and the results of their conversation. *(Homer is displeased when he realizes Sonny is studying calculus from his book. In response to Homer's inquiry about why he wants to learn calculus, Sonny tells him about Cape Coalwood and asks him to come see them. To Homer's reply that he might come when he has time, Sonny replies that he always has time for Jim. The ensuing confrontation reveals Homer's continuing desire for Sonny to become a mining engineer and his accusation that Sonny will do nothing Homer wants him to do. Sonny experiences inner conflict between what his father wants and his own dream. He begins to doubt his own vision of a future away from Coalwood. His anger toward Homer gives him the initiative to enter the science fair, knowing this will "show" his father. He decides he doesn't need his father's help and allows bitterness and anger to consume him. pp. 265–267, 270–273)*

Supplementary Activities

1. Divide the class into small groups and assign each group the preparation and presentation of a skit depicting one of the following confrontations: Homer vs. Elsie, the BCMA vs. state troopers, Sonny vs. Homer; Sonny and Quentin vs. Jim, Sonny vs. Mr. Turner. See Discussion Question #2 on page 26 of this guide for more information.

2. Literary Devices: **Similes**—Quentin nodded as if "he were a teacher who had finally gotten the correct response from the class dunce" (p. 263); I felt like "he'd handed me a big sackful of rocks" (p. 270) **Metaphor**—Sonny: other boys' ticket to college **Allusion**—Albert Einstein

Chapters 17–19, pp. 274–301

Valentine consoles Sonny after Dorothy dates Jim. Mr. Bykovski's death in a mine accident causes Sonny to temporarily abandon his rocket building. Mrs. Bykovski encourages Sonny to continue.

Vocabulary
syncopated (279)
translucent (281)
accolades (288)
converging (299)
diverging (299)

Discussion Questions

1. Discuss Valentine's role in Sonny's life. Elicit students' responses concerning her actions. *(Sonny attends a dance to get away from the intensity of rocket building. He is devastated when Dorothy arrives, and he realizes that she is the special date for which Jim had carefully prepared. As Sonny sees Dorothy "melt" in Jim's arms, Valentine asks Sonny to dance with her. He and Valentine leave, and Sonny has his first sexual encounter. Valentine, who recognizes his hurt over Dorothy, offers him her own love out of pity. pp. 274–283; Responses will vary.)*

2. Examine events surrounding the mine accident and the reactions of those involved. *(Lightning strikes two fans at the mine and causes sections of the mine to fall. Men are trapped and an explosion is imminent unless the fans are repaired soon. Homer insists on going into the mine against Elsie's urgent pleas. Sonny goes to the mine even though his mother has forbidden him to do so. A large group of people, including the doctor and the ministers, waits in fearful expectancy, speculating on the chances of the miners' survival. After breaking through to the miners, members of the rescue team bring to the surface the body of Isaac Bykovski. Sonny is devastated. Elsie arrives, but refuses to comfort Sonny, accusing him of being selfish. As other miners arrive on the surface, wives and children flock to them. Homer comes off the lift alone. He has a severe eye injury that causes him to lose sight in that eye. He walks home alone, with Elsie following. She rips the black phones from the wall. The doctor comes, tends to his injury, and tells Sonny and Jim that a dozen men would have died if it hadn't been for their dad. After his injury heals, Homer rarely comes home from the mine, and Elsie spends most of her time alone in her room. pp. 284–289, 299)*

3. Analyze Sonny's reaction to Bykovski's death. Elicit students' responses concerning the effects of guilt. *(He begins to cry and blames himself. Doc tells him to stop sniveling and reminds him that the men go each day into the mine, knowing they might die. He tells Sonny that Ike built the rockets for him because he wanted the best for him. Experiencing overwhelming guilt, Sonny feels that every door in Coalwood is slamming shut in his face. He realizes that he has been selfish all his life trying to make things go his way. He loses all energy and feels hopeless shame. He begins to feel sorry for himself, then suddenly realizes he feels nothing, the worst thing he has ever experienced. He quits building rockets, studying, and going to the machine shop. He avoids all contact with his parents and ignores everyone who tries to talk to him, including Dorothy and the Rocket Boys. He is scared but unable to admit it, even to himself. pp. 290–296; Responses will vary.)*

4. Examine what causes Sonny to emerge from his shroud of guilt. *(Miss Riley first causes him to feel something again when she asks about his not working on the rockets anymore. She tells him he is suffering from self-pity and pride. She tells him he must put all his hurt and anger aside so he can build rockets. Sonny goes to the bus stop to tell Mrs. Bykovski how sorry he is for her husband's death. She tells him that Ike could have gone back to the machine shop anytime he wished but didn't do so because they enjoyed the extra money. She urges him not to forget Ike and to honor him by continuing with his rockets, something Mr. Bykovski would have wanted Sonny to do. Sonny decides to continue building his rockets. pp. 295–298)*

Supplementary Activities
1. Add *Auk XXI* to the Rocket Chart.
2. Have students bring to class newspaper or magazine articles about recent mine disasters. Place these on a poster board and add others as students bring them.
3. Literary Devices: **Similes**—"waiting wives shuddered as if a cold wind had blown through them;" (Homer) walked away as if his "boots were made of lead" (p. 288); track bed looked like "an ugly black scar slashing through town" (p. 295)

Chapters 20–21, pp. 302–335

Sonny is seriously injured on a money-raising expedition with the Rocket Boys. The boys discover a more powerful propellant, and their rockets gain increasing height. The Company sells the miners' houses, and a new mine superintendent, Mr. Fuller, is hired. He attempts to shut down the BCMA's launch site, but Homer intervenes for Sonny and his friends.

Vocabulary
dulcet (304)
inanely (308)
quest (316)
covertly (316)
marauded (328)

Discussion Questions
1. Examine the Hickams' home life following the mine accident. Elicit students' responses as to how they would feel living in this type of atmosphere. *(Homer's eye does not heal properly. Homer and Elsie have reached a kind of peace but rarely speak to each other. Elsie is kind to Sonny but stays in her room a lot. The family rarely has dinner together, and Jim has nothing to do with Sonny. Only the pet cat, Daisy Mae, remains the same. pp. 302–303; Responses will vary.)*

2. Discuss the outcome of O'Dell's scheme to make money. *(O'Dell convinces the boys to help him dig up cast iron drainage pipes under the railroad track, telling them they can sell the pipes for scrap iron and make a ton of money. Sherman, Roy Lee, O'Dell, and Sonny go to the site to begin their excavations. The pipes are buried deeply, and it takes the boys five days to uncover one pipe. After two weeks, the boys have a large pile of scrap iron. Sonny slips, throws out his hand to catch himself, and slices an artery in his wrist. O'Dell saves his life by applying a tourniquet, and the four boys walk for six hours to get help. Sonny has lost a great deal of blood and is in shock. The doctor stitches his arm, and Sonny returns home. The boys sell the 400 pounds of scrap iron for $22.50. After paying off their debts, the BCMA is left without any profit from the adventure. pp. 305–311)*

3. Note the increasing audience for the rocket launches and the changes the boys continue to make to improve their rockets. *(About 100 people come to see the launch of* Auk XXII. *This is the first time the boys have used their zinc-sulfur propellants, and the rocket detonates on the launch pad. They begin to search for a better propellant, with the following results: A: breaks the mile barrier; B: flies erratically; C: bounces up and down in the tube; D: lands in Coalwood. pp. 312–315, 324–331)*

4. Discuss the recurring union/management conflict and its effects on Coalwood. *(The mine company decides to sell the miners' houses but will loan the miners the money to buy them. The mine management also plans to sell the churches and the utilities. Mr. Van Dyke is fired when he attempts to get the company to keep things as they are in Coalwood. The union threatens to strike. The temporary superintendent who replaces Van Dyke is Mr. Fuller. Fuller orders a big cut-off, and many miners lose their jobs. Dubonnet comes to the Hickam home, where he and Homer engage in an angry debate. pp. 313–315, 321–322)*

5. Discuss the development of zincoshine and its effects on rocket launches and on Sonny personally. Elicit students' responses concerning Sonny's bout with alcohol and how their parents would react. *(The boys decide to use alcohol to eliminate the air pockets in the zinc-sulfur powder. They go to John Eye's, the primary local moonshiner, to get their alcohol. John Eye insists that they have a drink of his liquor, and they all get drunk. Tag stops them on the way home and delivers each boy to his parents, but allows them to keep the moonshine when they explain why they bought it. The boys' experiments with zincoshine cause a hot water heater to blow up, but they finally perfect the propellant to their satisfaction, and Auk XXII–A soars 5,776 feet. In order to proceed with their next steps, the boys need to discover the thrust zincoshine produces. They change the way they launch the rockets, destroying the butcher's scale and Elsie's bathroom scale in the process. Auks XXII B–C fly erratically or not at all, but D lands in Coalwood. pp. 315–329; Responses will vary.)*

6. Discuss what happens to *Auk XXII–D* and its consequences. *(It lands in Coalwood, causing the general superintendent, Mr. Fuller, to become irate. Fuller orders the leveling of the BCMA's launch pad and erects a barbed wire fence around the site. Mr. Dubonnet and other miners defy Fuller's orders of no trespassing on the site, tear down the barbed wire, and rebuild the boys' blockhouse. When Fuller attempts to regain control, Homer forces him to back down. He then tells Sonny he can have anything he needs from the mine. pp. 332–335)*

7. Why does Homer stand up to Mr. Fuller, allowing the BCMA boys' launch pad to be rebuilt? How do you think his reaction affects Sonny? *(Responses will vary.)*

8. **Prediction:** Will Homer ever come to Cape Coalwood to watch Sonny launch a rocket?

Supplementary Activities

1. Add *Auks XXII A–D* to the Rocket Chart.

2. (a) Invite an EMT to come to class and relate life-saving techniques for the type of injury Sonny received or (b) Have students share with the class about a life-threatening accident they have had or know about personally.

3. Literary Devices: **Similes**—scrap iron "like gold" (p. 305); hornets "marauded up and down the slack like a tornado" (p. 328) **Allusion**—Apollo's fire: Apollo was the Greek mythological god of light (p. 326)

Chapters 22–23, pp. 336–383

Jim leaves for college. Economic conditions continue to deteriorate in Coalwood. The BCMA learns more about calculations for rocket construction, and they discover a money-making "gold mine" in a field of ginseng. Miss Riley reveals to Sonny that she has cancer. Sonny represents the BCMA in the McDowell County Science Fair and then at the area finals. The Rocket Boys win first place at both fairs, advancing them to the National Science Fair in Indianapolis. Homer and Elsie announce they are leaving Coalwood and moving to Myrtle Beach.

Vocabulary
adamantly (340)
protocol (348)
ginseng (350)
wan (362)
lymph nodes (362)
effusive (373)
intrepid (374)
ablative (374)

Discussion Questions

1. Discuss changes and major events in Sonny's life and in Coalwood during the 1959–60 school year. *(Suggestions: Jim leaves for college. Sonny is a senior. He ignores Dorothy but misses her friendship. Mr. Ferro produces anything Sonny needs for the BCMA. Miss Riley is ill with cancer. Big Creek's football team is off football suspension. Sonny, representing the BCMA, enters and wins the county and area science fairs, earning a trip to the national competition.)*

2. Examine the effect of the increasing union/company strife on the Hickam family. *(Mr. Fuller leaves Coalwood and is replaced by Mr. Bundini, who brings orders from the parent company for the mine to go on a four-day week. Homer becomes despondent after being forced to cut-off more men. Someone fires a gun at the Hickams' house, and someone runs over Daisy Mae and kills her. Elsie announces that they are going to Myrtle Beach to buy a house there. The union goes on strike, and Coalwood operations begin to suffer. At the BCMA's next rocket launch, union and company families stand apart. Throughout section)*

3. Discuss the progress of the BCMA's rocket building. *(The boys apply their skills at calculus and their practical knowledge toward developing a better rocket, especially in the rocket-nozzle design. They must make decisions concerning how fast and how high they want the rocket to go, then design the rocket to do so. Sonny relies on Quentin to make the calculations, but Quentin pushes Sonny to do them himself, and he does so successfully. Nearly three hundred people show up for the launching of Auk XXIII, which reaches 7,756 feet. Mr. Turner quizzes Sonny intently about rockets, and, to Miss Riley's delight, acknowledges that the boys' rocket project has an excellent chance of winning the science fair. pp. 336–345)*

4. Discuss the BCMA's winning entry in the county and area science fairs and the responses of those involved. *(County: Sonny and the other boys are afraid the judges will not give their entry, "A Study of Amateur Rocketry Techniques," a fair chance because they are from Big Creek High School. The judges make comments such as "Crazy," and "Looks to me like this could be really dangerous!" Sonny answers all questions without hesitation. After learning their project has won, Sonny is impatient to tell Miss Riley and his father. Homer is at the mine when Sonny gets home. Miss Riley is elated, and Mr. Turner is ready to place a bet on the next fair. The boys are the "Pride of the Hollows" and are asked to speak at civic clubs, where their grade school teachers beam with pride. Area: the boys once again win first place and will go to the National Science Fair. They also receive a first-prize certificate from the Air Force for being "Outstanding in the Field of Propulsion." The major who presents the award says that Sonny's display contains the most sophisticated rockets he has seen outside Cape Canaveral. Mr. Turner calls a school assembly to give the boys an encouraging send-off to Indianapolis. pp. 370–374, 377–380)*

5. Analyze Sonny's illness. Elicit students' responses as to whether Sonny is actually sick or if he is only suffering from nerves and stress. *(As the science fair approaches and tension in Coalwood between the union and the company intensifies, Sonny begins to experience nausea and headaches. After someone runs over Daisy Mae and kills her, Sonny blames himself for letting her out. He is overcome with emotion and becomes ill, vomiting profusely. On the way home from the area science fair, he again suffers from nausea and has a splitting headache. Sonny becomes disgusted with himself as the bouts of nausea and headaches continue. Sonny eventually releases his anger, finds closure for his grief, and discovers who he is and what he is going to do. His stomach and head immediately begin to feel better. pp. 367–368, 375, 379, 383; Responses will vary.)*

6. **Prediction:** Will Homer and Elsie move to Myrtle Beach?

7. **Prediction:** Will Miss Riley be able to finish the school year?

Supplementary Activities

1. Add *Auks XXIII–XXIV* to the Rocket Chart.

2. Have students bring to class and share pictures of special pets or write a short poem about a pet they lost.

3. Have students research the John F. Kennedy and Hubert Humphrey debates during the 1960 Presidential election and participate in an oral discussion.

4. Literary Devices: **Similes**—(Sonny) looked after Dorothy "like a lost puppy" (p. 337); "burned it out like it was cardboard" (p. 350); boys "look like some kind of silver turtle" (p. 354); mind felt as if it were being "sucked down into a whirlpool of red and white swirling blotches" (p. 376)

Chapter 24–Epilogue, pp. 384–428

The BCMA's rocket display wins the National Science Fair, and Sonny discovers his father's role in their success. The union/company fight is resolved, and the strike is ended. The group visits Miss Riley in the hospital and gives her their medal. The BCMA boys graduate from high school and launch their final rockets. Each one graduates from college. In retrospect Homer Hickam, Jr. recounts his career as a NASA engineer and relates his father's death.

Vocabulary

maria (390)
dictum (416)
parabola (418)

Discussion Questions

1. Examine Sonny's encounter with John F. Kennedy and analyze what this reveals about Kennedy and Sonny. Note: An article in the April 2003 *Reader's Digest* relates Kennedy's physical conditions that cause the symptoms Sonny observes, e.g., bronzed skin caused by Addison's disease and chronic back pain (see pages 388–389 of the novel). *(Kennedy is in Welch to make a speech the day Sonny goes to buy his suit. Sonny listens to him expound his views on government assistance for Appalachia. When Kennedy asks for questions from the audience, he acknowledges Sonny's hand, noticing him because of his new orange suit. In their dialogue about space, Sonny suggests the possibility of men going to the moon. The crowd responds with the first excitement they've shown during the speech. Kennedy affirms Sonny's suggestion. One of Kennedy's great dreams during his presidency was for the United States to go to the moon. pp. 389–391, 423)*

2. Discuss the required team effort and the complications Sonny encounters before and during the National Science Fair and how they are solved. Analyze Homer's sacrifice for his son and its ramifications. *(Team effort: Each boy of the BMCA contributes his skills toward making Sonny's presentation a success. Quentin drills Sonny incessantly the night before the trip. Complications: [1] Because of the union strike, Dubonnet grudgingly gives Caton special permission to build the necessary components for the rocket. [2] After arriving in Indianapolis, someone steals Sonny's nozzles, casements, and nose cones. He makes a frantic phone call home, asking for help. At first this seems impossible because of the intensification of the union/company strike, but Caton makes the parts, and they arrive in time for the judging. Sonny later learns that, in order to help him, Homer acceded to and signed Dubonnet's demands for the union in order to end the strike. Only then was Caton allowed to enter the welding shop and make the parts. Homer's signing the*

agreement necessitates his remaining in Coalwood, thus Elsie sacrifices her dream of moving to Myrtle Beach. [3] Tex and Sonny believe the propulsion exhibits have little chance of winning against the bigger, more expensive projects. Tex convinces the committee to place propulsion in its own separate category. pp. 393–411; Responses will vary.)

3. Analyze Jake's and Sonny's conversation about destiny. Elicit students' responses concerning whether or not they think our "fate" is preordained and to what degree we control our own destiny. *(Sonny is deeply troubled by Miss Riley's illness and thinks it is unfair for one so young to face an early death. Jake believes there is a plan for each person and it doesn't help to get angry with God about it. Sonny expresses a fear of the future and recalls the security he felt when, as a child, his father carried him upstairs. After learning the sequence of events leading to the settlement of the union/company dispute, Sonny recalls Jake's philosophy. He believes there is a supreme plan, and everyone eventually ends up where God wants him/her to be. pp. 405–406, 411; Responses will vary.)*

4. Examine the denouement and discuss the dreams that remain unfulfilled and those that are fulfilled. *(Unfulfilled: Sonny's love for Dorothy, whom he does not see again for 25 years after graduation. Fulfilled: On graduation night, Mr. Turner tells Sonny he has brought great honor to the school. The medal for the National Science Fair is placed in the trophy case. O'Dell, Billy, and Roy Lee join the Air Force, planning to attend college later on the GI Bill. Sonny, Sherman, and Quentin all make plans to attend college with varying types of financing. The boys decide to launch their final six rockets, and Elsie repeats her admonition, "Don't blow yourself up!" for the last time. A large crowd gathers to observe the highly successful launch of* Auks XXV–XXXI. *Homer arrives to view the final launch, and Sonny asks him to detonate the rocket. Sonny at last sees in his father the pride for which he has dreamed. pp. 407–421)*

5. Analyze why Sonny asks Homer to detonate the final rocket and why Homer reacts as he does. Note especially Homer's mixture of happiness, pain, and fear. *(When they realize Homer has come to watch the launch, all the BCMA boys insist they need his help. Sonny has longed for affirmation from his father all his life and recognizes the opportunity to include him in his dream. Sonny is delighted by the pure delight he sees in his father's face and in his reaction when the rocket soars almost six miles. Homer and Sonny reach a "moment of truth." Homer is happy for Sonny's success, pained because of the lost years of camaraderie with his son, and fearful of Sonny's reaction to him. Sonny, who has longed for his father to put his arm around his shoulder and tell him, at last, he has done something good, instead places his arm around Homer's shoulder and tells him no one ever launched a better rocket than he. pp. 419–421)*

6. Discuss Sonny Hickam's reflections in the Epilogue. *(He reveals the BCMA boys' success in college and their individual professions, Sherman's untimely death at 34, Jim's success as a coach, Sonny's renewed acquaintance with Dorothy, and Miss Riley's death at 32. His mother, and eventually his father, moved to Myrtle Beach, and his father died in 1989. The Coalwood mine shut down, never to be reopened. Homer Hickam, Jr. completed a successful and rewarding career with NASA, and the BCMA boys finally made it into space via one of the science fair medals and a piece of the Auk nozzle aboard the first trip of the space shuttle* Columbia. *pp. 421–427)*

Supplementary Activities

1. Add *Auks XXV–XXXI* to the Rocket Chart.

2. Have students write a letter to a teacher or other adult who has made a difference in their lives.

3. Literary Devices: **Similes**—eyes light up like "cats finding a bunny in the vegetable garden" (p. 386); trunk of fire and smoke tearing out of the mountains "like God's finger stuck suddenly toward the sky" (p. 420) **Allusion**—TVA project

Post-reading Discussion Questions

Note: Student responses will vary for the following questions. This section offers some suggested answers, with a detailed answer for question #5 for teacher's convenience.

1. Use the Sociogram on page 8 of this guide. Place Sonny Hickam's name in the center circle. In the surrounding circles, place the names Dorothy Plunk, Quentin, Jim Hickam, and Emily Sue Buckleberry. On the spokes surrounding each character's name, write several adjectives that describe that character. On the arrows joining Sonny and each character, describe the relationship between the two and discuss how one influences the other.

2. Using the Attribute Web on page 9 of this guide, write "The BCMA" in the center oval. In the surrounding boxes, write Sonny Hickam, Quentin, Elsie Hickam, Homer Hickam, Sr., Miss Riley, Jake Mosby, and a composite of Roy Lee, O'Dell, Sherman, and Billy. Discuss how each person relates to, assists, or hinders the goals of the BCMA.

3. Using the Story Map on page 10 of this guide, discuss the book.

4. Using the Understanding Values diagram on page 11 of this guide, discuss the values of characters from *October Sky*. Consider what they think is important, good, and worthwhile and list three important values for each character.

5. Complete the Rocket Chart on page 12 of this guide.
- #1: fuel in tube; blows up Elsie's fence; inadequate container for powerful fuel; different tubing, better fuel
- #2 [2 rockets]: aluminum tubing, black powder; 1st too weak, i.e., not enough powder—falls over without being airborne; 2nd too strong, i.e., too much powder; work on correct amount of powder
- *Auk I*: soldered aluminum body; flies 6 ft.; solder melts; Mr. Bykovski welds steel body
- *II–IV* launched same day; *II & III*: both fly erratically; *IV*: climbs smoothly; lands at the mine, Homer's wrath; modify powder
- *V–VIII* same design; *V*: climbs 50 ft., turns toward observers; powder too wet; for *VI–VIII*, cure powder longer; *VI*: streaks nearly out of sight; *VII*: horseshoe turn not more than 50 ft. up, slams into ground; *VIII*: bounces once, then explodes overhead; continue to search for best propellant, discover "rocket candy"
- *IX–XI* same design, same propellant; *IX*: dies quickly after takeoff; fuel burns too rapidly; pack fuel more efficiently; *X*: sits on pad and fizzles; wet fuel; *XI*: leaps off pad successfully, explodes; propellant collapses
- *XII & XIII*: both use melted rocket candy with electrical ignition system; *XII*: 760 ft.; *XIII*: unable to get accurate height but less than *XII*; both have corroded nozzles; search for material for nozzle that can withstand heat and oxidation
- *XIV & XV*: modified, thicker nozzle; *XIV*: 3,000 ft. *XV*: about 1,500 ft.
- *XVI–XIX*: using stronger nozzle, all perform flawlessly—two-footers, about 3,000 ft., three-footers, 2,000 ft.
- *XX*: same design; climbs 300 ft. and explodes; too much sustained pressure; need seamless tubing
- *XXI*: 4,100 ft; decide to use zinc dust and sulfur for propellant
- *XXII A–D*: seamless tubing, alcohol added to propellant; *A*: 5,776 ft; *B*: throws out plume of flame and smoke, whizzes about erratically; *C*: bounces up and down; *D*: high and straight, lands in Coalwood; continue to refine modifications
- *XXIII*: first based on mathematical equations and scientific theories; 7,056 ft.
- *XXIV*: 8,500 ft.
- *XXV*: 15,000 ft.
- *XXVI–XXXI*: all launched the same day, each with slightly different design and size; ranges from 3,000 ft. to nearly 6 miles high

6. Analyze the different types of conflict in the memoir and whether or not they are resolved. *(Homer, Sr. vs. Elsie; Homer vs. Sonny and the BCMA; Jim vs. Sonny; the BCMA vs. law enforcement; the BCMA vs. Mr. Turner; Sonny's conflict with himself; union vs. company; Responses will vary.)*

7. Examine the significance of the "truths" Sonny discovers after he begins to build and launch rockets (page 1 of the novel) and correlate with the events. *(Truths: His hometown was at war with itself over its children; his parents were locked in combat about how he and his brother would live their lives; if a girl broke your heart, another could mend it; how to transform enthalpy decrease into jet kinetic energy. Significance: Coalwood was locked into the mentality that Big Creek High School was predominantly for athletics, yet some parents dreamed of a better life for their children. Sonny's father expected Sonny to follow him into the mine, yet his mother was determined he would escape that life. When Dorothy broke his heart, Valentine consoled him intimately. Sonny learned to apply the study of upper-level mathematics and science to the development of rockets and to produce the energy necessary for rocket launches.)*

8. Examine the effectiveness of the memoir genre. *(Suggestions: allows the narrator to reflect events and emotions; can be correlated to historical events; reader becomes involved vicariously; characters presented just as narrator remembers them)*

9. Analyze "dreams" in the memoir and whether or not these dreams are fulfilled. *(Sonny: Dorothy, building rockets; Elsie: dream of a more serene life, e.g., depicted by mural; the BCMA boys: college; Miss Riley: success of her students; Homer: Jim getting a football scholarship, Sonny becoming a mining engineer)*

10. Examine the importance of the setting of the novel. *(Responses will vary, but should include references to the "space race" with Russia, JFK's political agenda, NASA's emergence, etc.)*

11. Analyze the development of themes in the novel. *(Example: perseverance—determination to find new way to launch rockets, better fuel, learn math/science; Sonny's determination to get good grades and take advanced courses to learn all he can)*

Post-reading Extension Activities

Writing
1. Prepare a time line, breaking your life into incremental steps of 3 years, revealing your memories of each 3-year segment. Project an additional span of 12 years showing your dreams/plans for the future.
2. Write a letter from Sonny to Miss Riley five years after his high school graduation.
3. Write a eulogy for Homer Hickam, Sr.
4. Write a poem about someone you know who has the same attributes as Sonny.

Art/Photography
5. Create a collage of scenes around Coalwood, West Virginia.
6. Draw a series of sketches showing the development of the rockets.
7. Produce a picture essay of one teacher or a composite of several teachers with attributes similar to Miss Riley. Take photos depicting these attributes, in or out of the classroom, and add appropriate captions.

Drama/Music
8. Write a TV script for the mine tragedy scene. Select and play appropriate music as you stage the scene.
9. Write and stage a TV script for the final rocket scene. Select and play appropriate background music.

Viewing
10. View the movie *October Sky*, and then give an oral report comparing/contrasting the movie with the book.

Current Events
11. Select and bring to class pictures of or articles about coal-mining towns.
12. Select and bring to class articles relating to current space exploration in the United States. Note especially articles about the February 1, 2003, destruction of the space shuttle *Columbia* and ensuing articles about NASA's future plans.

Assessment for *October Sky*

Assessment is an ongoing process. The following items can be completed during the novel study. Once finished, the student and teacher will check the work. Points may be added to indicate the level of understanding.

Name _____ Date _____

Student	Teacher	
_____	_____	1. Write four review questions, two that reflect knowledge of the book, e.g., "When...," "What..." and two that reflect analysis, e.g., "Compare...," "What caused..."
_____	_____	2. Correct all quizzes taken over the novel.
_____	_____	3. For small group work, the teacher will assign you one or two of the following people: Quentin; Basil Oglethorpe; Jake Mosby; Homer Hickam, Sr.; Elsie Hickam; Miss Riley; Isaac Bykovski; Clinton Caton. Evaluate his or her contributions to Sonny's realization of his dream through the BCMA. Share your evaluation with the rest of the class.
_____	_____	4. Write a critique of the book for the school newspaper.
_____	_____	5. Compare/contrast your completed character charts, story maps, and comprehension activities with a partner. Write a short essay explaining the areas for which each listed different information and why.
_____	_____	6. Display or perform your Post-reading Extension project on the assigned day.
_____	_____	7. Write a riddle about one of the characters and have the class try to identify your character.
_____	_____	8. As a class assignment, conduct a TV interview with Homer Hickam, Jr. about his life as a Rocket Boy and later as a NASA engineer. The teacher will appoint students to fill the roles of Hickam and the interviewer. The rest of the class will represent members of the press.
_____	_____	9. As the teacher calls out various themes found in the book, write the name of one person or one situation that demonstrates that theme.

Glossary

Chapter 1, pp. 1–16
1. enthalpy (1): the heat content per unit mass of substance
2. kinetic (1): of or having to do with motion
3. bituminous coal (1): soft, black coal that burns with much smoke and yellow flame
4. sonorous (4): giving out or having a deep, rich sound
5. pristine (7): original; primitive; as it was in earliest state
6. tipple (11): a place where freight cars and mining cars are tipped and emptied

Chapter 2, pp. 17–44
1. precipitously (26): steeply; rapidly
2. prowess (33): unusual skill or ability
3. proclivity (33): tendency; inclination
4. inexorable (39): relentless; unyielding
5. molecule (39): smallest particle into which a substance can be divided without chemical change

Chapters 3–4, pp. 45–70
1. impotent (55): not having power; helpless
2. entity (62): something that has a real and separate existence
3. surreptitiously (65): acting stealthily or secretly

Chapter 5, pp. 71–87
1. oxidizer (74): a substance that supports the combustion of a fuel
2. succinctly (77): expressed briefly and clearly
3. insidious (78): crafty; underhanded; more dangerous than is apparent
4. cohesiveness (78): sticking together
5. saltpeter (79): a white, salty mineral used in making gunpowder
6. casement (83): covering; frame

Chapters 6–7, pp. 88–128
1. nefarious (94): very wicked; villainous
2. propellant (98): explosive fuel and oxidizer that projects a rocket
3. prodigious (100): wonderful; amazing; tremendous
4. pernicious (104): fatal; deadly; causing great harm or damage
5. cupidity (105): greed
6. cogitative (106): thoughtful; meditative
7. subjective (119): about thoughts and feelings, e.g., opinions are subjective; facts are objective
8. rabble-rouser (121): a person who tries to stir up people with inflammatory speeches; agitator
9. petulance (124): testiness, bad humor; condition of being irritated by trifles

Chapters 8–9, pp. 129–162
1. ballistic missile (129): a projectile aimed before the time of launch that is forced into a high arch and then free-falls in its descent
2. debacle (136): sudden downfall or collapse; disaster

3. polyhedron (152): a solid figure having four or more faces
4. ironic (162): contrary to (opposite of) what is expected or intended

Chapters 10–11, pp. 163–205
1. deductive (169): logical reasoning; inferable
2. infinity (169): condition of being infinite, i.e., endless
3. coalescing (170): growing or fusing together; uniting
4. primordial (184): existing at very beginning; primitive
5. viscous (186): thick and sticky, like glue or heavy syrup
6. slurry (187): semi-fluid substance
7. theodolite (190): surveying instrument for measuring horizontal and vertical angles
8. methane (194): colorless, odorless, flammable gas

Chapters 12–13, pp. 206–245
1. truncated (207): cut off
2. tensile (213): having to do with tension
3. aperture (214): opening; gap
4. parameters (217): measurable factors which help other such factors to define a system

Chapters 14–16, pp. 246–273
1. thermodynamics (248): branch of physics that deals with the relations between heat and other forms of energy
2. isentropic (248): of or having to do with a constant or equal entropy; i.e., a measure of the degree of disorder of a system
3. adiabatic (248): occurring without loss or gain of heat
4. elliptical (253): shaped like an ellipse, i.e., an oval having both ends alike
5. trajectories (253): curved paths
6. overt (254): open; evident; not hidden
7. ebullience (257): lively enthusiasm
8. flange (268): raised edge
9. guile (273): deceit; craftiness

Chapters 17–19, pp. 274–301
1. syncopated (279): characterized by syncopation, i.e., shifting of accent to a normally unaccented beat
2. translucent (281): transparent; letting light through
3. accolades (288): awards; honors
4. converging (299): centering; meeting on a point
5. diverging (299): moving in different directions

Chapters 20–21, pp. 302–335
1. dulcet (304): soothing; sweet or pleasing
2. inanely (308): foolishly; senselessly
3. quest (316): search; hunt
4. covertly (316): hidden
5. marauded (328): searched for plunder; raided

Chapters 22–23, pp. 336–383
1. adamantly (340): firmly; resolutely
2. protocol (348): rules for a procedure
3. ginseng (350): plant with aromatic root that is used in herbal medicines
4. wan (362): pale, faint, weak; looking worn or tired
5. lymph nodes (362): glands in the body that filter out bacteria and other harmful microorganisms from lymph
6. effusive (373): too demonstrative and emotional; talkative
7. intrepid (374): fearless; courageous; dauntless
8. ablative (374): made to be removed by ablation, i.e., the removal or carrying away of heat by melting or vaporization

Chapter 24–Epilogue, pp. 384–428
1. maria (390): a broad, flat, dark area on the moon
2. dictum (416): a formal comment; authoritative opinion
3. parabola (418): a plane curve formed by the intersection of a cone with a plane parallel to the side of the cone